Birth

When the Spiritual and
the Material Come Together

SHARI ARISON

PHOENIX
BOOKS

ISBN-13: 978-1-60747-725-9
ISBN-10: 1-60747-725-4

Library of Congress Cataloging-in-Publication Data available.

Printed in the United States of America

Phoenix Books, Inc.
9465 Wilshire Boulevard, Suite 840
Beverly Hills, CA 90212

10 9 8 7 6 5 4 3 2 1

*For my mother, and father of blessed memory,
who gave me life.
For my children Jason, David, Cassie, and Daniel:
You light up my world. You are the greatest gift
in my life. I love you very, very much.*

About the Author

Shari Arison is an American-Israeli businesswoman and philanthropist. Arison is repeatedly ranked by *Forbes* magazine as one of the world's wealthiest women and was also ranked by *Forbes* among the top 50 most influential women in the world in 2008.

Shari Arison was born in the United States (1957) and is the daughter of Mina Arison Sapir and the late American-Israeli businessman Ted Arison, the founder of Carnival Cruise Lines.

Shari Arison has a significant beneficial interest in Carnival Corporation and has served twice on its board of directors.

She leads the Arison Group, a business and philanthropic group. The Group's business arm is made up of leading corporations including Bank Hapoalim, Israel's largest bank; Shikun & Binui, one of the largest real estate and infrastructures companies in Israel; and Salt Industries, the largest salt manufacturer in Israel. She is also the founder of Miya, the Arison Group's global water company.

The Group's philanthropic arm includes among others the Ted Arison Family Foundation, which addresses the needs of the community, and Essence of Life, an organization whose aim is to heighten awareness and provide tools for attaining inner peace, both in Israel and abroad. Shari Arison also initiated the annual Good Deeds Day, which each year gives people the opportunity to volunteer and help others.

In 2005, she was named as an Honorary Fellow of the Decade at the Interdisciplinary Center Herzliya, and she has been serving as a board member there since 2007.

In both 2007 and 2009, Shari Arison was chosen as Woman of the Year by *Globes*, one of Israel's leading financial newspapers.

Shari Arison is the mother of four and currently resides in Israel.

Please visit: www.arison.com

Exposing oneself is always frightening and difficult, especially when it entails exposing the soul, the inner self. There is always the fear that people will not accept what you have to offer, that they will laugh at you, pass judgment on you, or perhaps even worse.

My need to bare my soul to the world emanates from the Talmudic verse that states: "…whoever saves one life is considered as if he had saved the entire world." (Jerusalem Talmud, Mishnah Sanhedrin 4:5)

I feel a great need to help humanity. I wish to inspire a change in people. I want to bring people closer to God. And if my exposure accomplishes this, then the fear—and the difficulty it entails—are worth the risk.

Table of Contents

Birth

THE OLD WORLD IS COLLAPSING AROUND US. THE PERSONAL, THE INTERPERSONAL, THE MATERIAL, THE ENVIRONMENTAL, AND THE POLITICAL—THEY ARE ALL NOW IN A STATE OF FLUX, OF VOLATILITY, OF CHANGE. We are facing a new world, a world we have never known before. A world in which the familiar laws and traditional perceptions will no longer be of help to us. A world in which the conventional differences between the economic-business-material and the spiritual is no longer valid. We are facing a world in which the spiritual and the material come together.

The old world is collapsing around us. Not all at once, but in a process that started several years ago and is now reaching its climax. Like a wound that needs to be cleansed in order to heal, this climax is also accompanied by pain and suffering, by an infection that must be purged. This purging burns, causes pain, but this pain is essential. So that we can begin anew, we need to cleanse ourselves from what we do to ourselves, from what we do to each other, from what we do to our environment and to our world. The ever-growing aggression, the erupting wars, the collapsing economy, the poisoned air, the hostile media, the raging epidemics—all the plagues of the world are our infection. It is from these that we must free ourselves and heal ourselves in order to reach the new, the clean, the altered.

For too long humanity has acted with an outrageous lack of responsibility. We lost our balance and shifted our world out of balance. We wanted everything for ourselves. We failed to look at the overall picture and did not take into consideration those with whom we share the world—other human beings, living creatures, the earth and its resources, the entire planet. We focused only on ourselves. We took everything for granted and thought that the world was meant to serve us, that everything in it was created for us, and that all of it would still be here tomorrow. This arrogance has led us to the point where we are destroying our world—in every way, and not just environmentally—with our very own hands.

I believe we must understand that if we want change, we must create change. It is not in the hands of governments, nor in the hands of leaders or gurus, nor in the hands of the powerful or the wealthy. It is in *our* hands, the hands of each and every one of us. All of us have a share in the future, at every level: personally, interpersonally, politically, economically, and environmentally. Everyone must focus on his or her part, whether they are businesspeople or farmers, high-tech workers or schoolteachers. We must find our essence, to understand, to accept, and to respect first ourselves and then the Other, to contribute our part.

For most of my life I have received messages—images and worded communications, sometimes even in an ancient language—that come to me from above. In the past, I used the help of channelers who interpreted the messages for me, but today I know how to receive those messages directly, without the need for interpretation, without the inevitable bias that takes place when information passes through someone else's filters (to stress this point, I use in this book two different words to describe the same phenomenon: "channeling"—given to me by another, and "message"— communicated to me directly).

About two years ago, I received a message in which I was told to prepare myself for an impending collapse. My response was not economic; I did not rush to sell my assets in order to prevent losses or try to make a profit. My only response was to continue with even greater determination on my path, on the path that I and the companies in the Arison Group have followed in recent years: a powerful and decisive process aimed at realizing the Group's vision.

My purpose in this book is to share the path I have traveled, in the spiritual realm and in the business realm, to share the insights I have reached regarding the essential connection between the two, to speculate as to the nature of the new world we are approaching, and to reveal my business-spiritual model—a new model for a new world, which will enable individuals, companies, and even states and nations to transform the collapse all around us into change, and to bring together the spiritual and the material, and from this meeting, give birth to a new future.

Spirit

L IKE A RESEARCHER WHO DEDICATES HIS OR HER LIFE TO AN EFFORT TO HEAL ILLNESSES OR DISCOVER NEW STARS, I SEE MYSELF AS A RESEARCHER. A researcher of the self. My research deals with consciousness, essence, and the discovery of new ways to reach them. There are countless paths for learning the lessons of life, and I have walked on many of them. Some of them are rocky and hard, some have many traffic lights, and some are like highways. All of these paths have ultimately led me to myself. But even on the fastest roads, the path is not easy. There are many challenges along the way, and you need patience, willpower, and faith to regroup and continue on, even if you fall—and always, at some stage, you will fall because there is nothing perfect except for God. And when we become perfect, we will finally be united with God. Our goal in this life is to try to achieve perfection, try to transform, and there are many transformations to be made. When one ends, we move on to the next one.

Am I a religious person? Some say that I am more religious than religious people. But in my eyes, religion and spirituality are two different things. I believe that religion, as an institution, is divisive. We must rise above religions and see that we are all in fact one. We are all part of the same whole. It is possible to be a religious person without being connected to oneself, to one's essence. And it is possible to be a non-religious person who is very connected, and vice versa. The meaning of this connection is closeness to and acquaintance with the divine spark that is within each and every one of us, the spark that is the source, the essence and inner beauty. The family in which I grew up, for example, was very secular but also extremely Jewish. And I have always been connected to the Jewish tradition and to a feeling that

Judaism has a mission to fulfill in this world, that we can bring *tikkun olam* (transformation) to the world.

Around the year 1996, I met a channeler who told me that everything we know is about to change, and that I have a role in what is about to unfold, that I am destined to lead the people of Israel. It was very difficult for me to hear this, and I did not really understand what she meant. But during the ensuing years, after many other things she told me about my businesses and my late father's businesses came to fruition, and after much inner consciousness work that I did with myself, I have learned to accept the future she saw for me. Today, I believe that I do indeed have a mission in this world, a mission to lead and to guide. Not out of vanity and not from political aspiration—but out of the understanding that I have the tools to bring change to the world, and that I have the ability to envision this change, to see the vision of the new world, and to influence people. And that I can use my personal example to show the way.

Even during my childhood, I always felt ill at ease in the world. I felt that perhaps I did not belong, that something in me or in the world was wrong and lacking. I already knew then, even before I could put my feelings into words, that we had lost our way. The violence, the suffering, the cruelty that I saw in the world were immense, and I felt that they were contrary to the true essence of humanity. To our divine essence. As I grew up, I understood that although I felt out of place, my mission—my purpose in life, the reason for my existence—was to help people, humanity, the world, to reach the true essence.

Today I feel the old collapsing within me. I feel that while great transformations occur in the world, an enormous change is also happening within me. All of the feelings of guilt, insult, loneliness, lack of self-esteem, lack of confidence, sadness, depression, pain—all these are collapsing within me and are being released, making room for understanding and tranquility, for self-acceptance, for freedom and abundance, for love. I have always believed and felt that the external reality is a reflection of me, of us, of each of us. And therefore, the external collapse we see around us is also an internal collapse. And if we learn how to reach our true essence, this will also be reflected in our external reality.

I began my emotional and spiritual journey as a frightened and angry child who did not know how to express her feelings. I grew up in a home where emotions were not dealt with, or talked about, in which I felt my own emotions were being suppressed and denied. It took me years to find my voice and begin using it. Even then, I had a great sensitivity for what is to come. I felt and sometimes saw things before they happened, and I felt a great connection with what lies beyond the simple everyday reality. When I tried to tell people about the things I experienced, they did not believe me and told me, "There are no such things." The gap between what I knew to be the truth, which I saw with my eyes and felt in my body, and the lack of faith of the people around me, generated a difficult feeling within me that only years later I was able to identify as fear.

This sensitivity and differentness, especially in a family like mine that was not attentive to these matters, generated friction and problems during my childhood and youth, and my parents turned to conventional psychology to try to find solutions. My first encounter with therapy was traumatic: a psychologist who treated me violated the privilege between us and spoke with my mother about the issues we had discussed during our sessions.

Other encounters were no less difficult: I was ten years old when my father remarried, and there was great anger within me that I did not know how to handle. I wanted to kill my stepmother. I actually sat and planned how I would get rid of her. At age twelve, my parents took me for treatment to a psychologist who specialized in the Gestalt method, a very dramatic and shocking technique for me. In our first session, the therapist lay on the floor and invited me to kill her. "Kill me!" she told me. "Show me how you would kill me. You can choke me if you want. Show me how you're going to do it." Of course, I could not do anything, and the shock of the incident completely dissolved my anger. "One day," she told me, "you will have to deal with your fears." At the time, I did not understand what she meant because, as I said, I couldn't identify the feelings I experienced as fears. In the fullness of time I came to understand what she meant.

Today, of course, I have a wonderful relationship with Lin, my father's widow, and we love and respect each other very much.

These experiences taught me to be suspicious of psychology. The trust that was violated and the shock of the Gestalt therapy left a deep mark within me, created layers, a scar tissue in my soul. This fear, however, did not prevent me from taking great interest in the field, and I even considered studying psychology at one point, before I started college in the United States. I did not lose this curiosity, and when I returned to Israel in the summer of 1991, I studied psychology at the Open University. The experience I had undergone, and what I had managed to learn about the field, made it clear to me that while conventional treatment is beneficial to some people, I am not one of them. I do not reject any method, of course. But I think that each method should be adapted to the individual.

In my twenties, following crises in my personal life, I began to participate in support groups. For the first time in my life, I was part of a group of people who struggled with problems that were similar to mine, and I learned a lot about mutual support. I participated in sessions for a very long time, and they helped me to understand that I am not alone and that I must accept responsibility for my part in whatever difficult situation I am in. At the time, I could only understand the importance of this responsibility rationally. I was very young. I cannot say that I truly understood it in depth, because during the course of my life I found myself repeating the same mistakes over and over and over, and I am still struggling with them today, but in other ways.

There are things in our lives that we understand better at every stage we pass. But the beginning of my path, my initial learning of responsibility, I did there, in the support groups.

After Jason, my eldest son, was born, I began to develop profound fears, very severe phobias. The maternal, protective impulse transformed the fears I had experienced since my childhood, which only now I could identify, into phobias. When I was alone, I could cope with the fear. I could tell myself that even if something happened to me, it would not be so terrible. But the moment the children were born, everything became more frightening. My maternal instinct was so overwhelming that I was afraid of everything. I was afraid of crowded places. I would go to a movie theater or enter a supermarket, and if there were too many people around me, I would become stressed and faint. The doctors told me that I had hypoglycemia and low blood pressure—my soul and my body worked in tandem. I was afraid of heights. If we climbed a mountain on a trip, I would become hysterical. The worst phobia concerned flying. Even today, after I have done a great amount of work with myself in this area, I think and calculate thousands of times before I decide to fly. But back then my condition was much more severe. All my life, I have flown very frequently between the United States and Israel, and my life has been split between these two places. But nonetheless, I did not board a plane during the first five years of Jason's life. I could not. I was scared to death. Hypnosis enabled me to attempt to fly, but it did not solve the problem. I would sit fifteen hours in coach class with three small children, clutching the seat and crying. I explained to the children that they should not talk to me because I could not cope with the fear. I often wondered what power compelled me to continue to try, and today I know that I have enormous willpower that has accompanied me throughout life and enabled me to improve, to change, to succeed, and in particular—to come to Israel.

I understood that I must deal with this distress, that these phobias were causing me to miss out on significant things in my life, that I needed to do self-work that would liberate me. During that period, I read *Many Lives, Many Masters*, a book by the psychiatrist Dr. Brian Weiss, which deals with the possibility of reincarnation and its psychological impact on a person. I was very impressed by his ideas and requested a meeting with him. The first meeting left a very profound impression on me, and the things Dr. Weiss said about the possibilities of the soul before it chooses to arrive in the body resonated deeply within me.

When I returned to Israel in 1991, I wanted to continue to participate in support groups, but the feeling there was different; although the groups were built according to American models, I felt uncomfortable. In the United States, there was always a feeling that the confidentiality of the participants was sacred, and I never feared that things would be divulged beyond the boundaries of the group. In Israel, I did not feel this security. I continued to search for my path on my own, and after I read another book by Dr. Weiss, *Through Time Into Healing,* I decided that the next stop in my path would be with him. I wrote him a letter, but by that point he was already very famous and did not accept new patients. He traveled the world, wrote books, was interviewed on television. But I got lucky and thanks to our single meeting, many years before, he contacted my personal assistant in Miami and agreed to see me.

I arrived in Miami for two very emotional and intensive weeks. I asked Dr. Weiss to conduct a session every day during my stay, but he would not agree to this under any circumstances and informed me that he would be willing to see me just once. But that one session stretched into twelve sessions, each one centering on a different incarnation. And during one of them, I even experienced death—I saw a surge of light that flooded everything and, in the distance, a glowing corridor where a messenger stood, awaiting me. The experience was dramatic. At first, I thought I was simply imagining things. Hallucinating. But I began to discern the abundance of details, and the details that I could not understand or identify—the things that belonged to my previous incarnations, which I, in this life, was totally unaware of. I have learned that nothing ends with death and that if I do not deal with issues, resolve them, and let them go, they might resurface in another incarnation.

During these meetings, Dr. Weiss told me that one day I will be extremely important to world peace, but at the time I did not understand what he was talking about, and I could not cope with the idea. For a year, I did not speak about the sessions with Dr. Weiss. The experience was so strong that I feared that people would think I was crazy. I was afraid to tell, but when I returned to Israel I felt that I had to continue to investigate the spiritual and soulful sides of me and of the world. At that time, there was no focused desire behind my searching, such as the desire for support, which had led me to the support groups, or the desire to deal with my phobias, which had led me to regression therapy and to Dr. Weiss. Instead, the desire went deeper. I was searching for answers. I have always had a strong desire to advance, to know, to learn, precisely in these realms. The search for more and more knowledge focused on the "unconventional" world. The academic world turned me off. I had met so many teachers who knew less than me about the true lessons that life teaches us, and despite this they presumed to teach me. I objected to the notion that the diploma makes the person. Today I understand that deep down I feared that I would not succeed. I feared that I was not good enough. I was afraid that I would not be able to concentrate. I am sure that today I would be diagnosed with some sort of learning disability because I see the difficulty myself. It was easier for me to reject than to confront. I still think that the diploma does not make the person, but I now respect people who pursue this path. I freed myself from the contempt I felt—contempt that stemmed, I believe, from the wrong place.

At a relatively early stage in my path, I already believed that when I was ready the right teacher would arrive. And indeed, during seventeen years of searching and learning, I have moved from one teacher to another and from one method to another, knowing that at the right time and place, when I was ready—someone would come.

In the course of time, I experienced, studied, and was treated with many theories, and I felt that every method I was exposed to was correct for its time. Even if I left it behind and continued onward, I took something of it away with me, understood something, recognized my points of strength and weakness, familiarized myself with concepts that would become essential in my life, and ascended to a higher level of consciousness—of the body, of the spirit, and of the soul.

There were fields that I studied in only a basic or partial way, up to the point where I felt that I had found what I was looking for, taken what I could and continued onward, such as A Course in Miracles, The Silva Method, and The Forum. There were methods I used for years on a weekly basis, until the conclusion of the process, such as "rebirthing," healing—raising frequencies, Shiatsu, acupuncture, and more. And there were fields that I pursued in depth, such as Chi Kung, Reiki, and various forms of meditation. I studied different approaches in the area of Kabbalah, including Kabbalist meditation. During the six months that I practiced it, I was full of light; I had so much energy that I could, literally, dance all night. I felt that I could do anything. But slowly, I began to feel that I had not yet reached a high enough level of consciousness, that I was still not clean enough to use the power that Kabbalist meditation allows for my personal use, for my enjoyment, for my needs. I stopped practicing it, and despite feeling a great loss, as if all the light was extinguished, I knew, deep in my heart, that I took the right step, that I was still not ready for all this light.

Today I know that when one reaches the true essence, there is no longer a need for meditation. Meditation is important when there are layers, but after cleansing them away and freeing oneself from them, there is no longer a need for a method, a technique that enables contact with our deepest inner self. But there is no need, of course, to stop the in-depth observation and connecting with ourselves.

I have always tried to reach a balance between the material and the spiritual. Thus, among the methods I experienced were some that focus on the body, some that focus on the spirit, and some that utilize both. In one of the messages I received, I was told that the body is the temple of the soul, and since then I try to nurture, respect, and guard my temple—from inside and from outside. I do not always succeed, of course.

And, like everyone, I also have slip-ups, moments when I lose control, periods of unhealthy eating, of neglect. But I always try to engage in a broad range of sports and try to maintain a healthy diet within the restrictions of my vegetarian lifestyle, a practice which became absolute after I visited Africa. It was there that I understood nature; I understood that every creature is a creature of God. The colors, the sunrises, the sunsets, the freedom, the animals— all this opened my soul. One day, I went out to feed the giraffes at a ranch in Kenya, and in a restaurant that evening they served us a delicacy—giraffe. From that moment on, I have not touched any meat. Several years later, I learned about the Jain sect in India. In one of their ceremonies, I saw how they walk with a broom and sweep the earth in front of them in order to avoid harming any living creatures, not even killing an ant by mistake. From that day onwards, I stopped using leather.

These experiences, and a book called *Mutant Message Down Under* by Marlo Morgan, which tells of an American woman's experiences with a tribe of Aboriginal Australians, has shaped my attitude towards nature.

Today, I do not use anything that causes suffering to an animal—I do not wear leather clothes or shoes, do not adorn myself with pearls, and do not eat meat. When I look into the eyes of an animal, I feel that I see its soul, the life force in its eyes, and I am not willing to take this life force from it.

While engaging in spiritual and physical work, I continued to have the same experiences that accompanied me since my childhood—my ability to see the future grew stronger. I saw things before they happened, and this frightened me very much. The knowledge of what is about to happen is always accompanied by very painful and powerful physical sensations. When missiles are fired at Israeli cities, at Tel Aviv in the 1991 Gulf War or at Sderot today, I feel this in my bones. I feel that I am on fire, mourning the losses that are not mine and have yet to occur. During one of my vacations, in Turkey, my husband and I sat on the deck of the yacht with friends when I suddenly started to cry bitterly. I told my husband that I saw a huge wave and thousands of people about to die in the sea. It was an awful feeling of helplessness. What can I do? Would anyone believe me? Is it true? To my horror, it turned out that my premonition was correct this time as well because two months later the tsunami hit Southeast Asia. The same thing happened with Hurricane Katrina and many other disasters.

For years, I suffered greatly from these visions, sensations, and messages, which were examined again and again and had always become a reality. I prayed that they would disappear. They brought a lot of pain to my life. It was difficult to share them with those around me who did not understand or accept and regarded my authentic experiences with disdain or disbelief. Today I know that this was precisely the reason why I received them—so that I would learn to rely on myself and believe in myself, in what I see and feel. This was preparation for the current stage—a stage in which I am ready to come forward and declare what I know, with courage and without fear.

Recently, the messages that I receive have changed. There is still pain, but happily, it is dissipating. In the past, the visions were always harsh, catastrophic and violent. But I have recently been able to see the new world—the quiet, the tranquility, and the freedom it will bring with it. This is very comforting knowledge for me because I already know that what I envision eventually becomes a reality.

Another teaching that influenced me in a significant way was that of the Brahma Kumaris, a group that originated in India and seeks to promote world peace, self-knowledge, and spiritual growth—but through a deep connection to the realistic world. A very well-established group, Brahma Kumaris has a delegation at the UN, centers around the world, and connections with the business community and media. In every community in which they operate, they teach how to take their tools and use them within the community or business. They taught me a lot about my soul, about meditational ways through which it is possible to connect to the soul, to cleanse it of evil, and to connect to the good within. For many years, whenever I was in their company, I felt like I had come home. At one point in my studies, I even took with me the leaders of this method in Israel, the director of the center and my personal teacher, and traveled to meet Dadi Janki, their spiritual leader. But I ultimately came to the conclusion that they are primarily connected to the soul, and, as noted, the connection to the body is very important for me. I also did not share their belief in a guru. I know that many people, even those around me, sometimes say, "Oh, look, Shari has found herself a new guru." But I do not believe in the idea of a guru and have never adopted a guru. I meet teachers, learn with them and from them, and when I feel that I have learned all I can, I move on to study something new from another teacher. This type of process has always been accepted in the academic world, where you study, delve into, and investigate in your field, and then can decide to examine and explore another subject. But there the teacher who guides you in your studies is called a professor, and it is acceptable to move through different levels of interest and different degrees of study. In the academic world, this is accepted and expected, while in the spiritual world such teachers are called "gurus," and those who do not understand this practice are afraid of them and their influence.

One of the most significant things for anyone who is interested in engaging in spiritual work with himself is to know when the path he is pursuing is leading him to bad places. For example, there was a channeler I left because at a certain stage I felt that the connection between us had become unclean. I felt that she was starting to give me manipulative messages. That was the point at which I discontinued the connection with her.

You always need to examine where you are in relation to the person opposite you within the spiritual process, and to remember that the things that make you feel better do not always bring you closer to your essence. In one of the incidents I experienced, I worked with someone who was able to make me feel powerful, but not necessarily in the good sense of the word. I noticed that I was feeling very good and doing things that perhaps I would not have allowed myself to do in the past, including business moves that I once did not have the courage to do, like making changes, being decisive, letting people go. But, on the other hand, I was moving farther away from my essence.

The process led me to a place in which I was very strong, where I could take action without feeling. I did not care about anyone. And I felt excellent.

As a person who experiences life—her own and those of others—with enormous sensitivity, who is profoundly aware of the feelings of others and thinks of others more than herself, there was something very liberating about this process. Suddenly, for the first time in my life, I did not see anyone. I did not care about anyone. I was only interested in what I wanted.

I learned a lot from this experience. I realized that perhaps I had to go from one extreme to another before I could find balance. Everything we experience, everything we undergo in our lives, has its own reasons. I do not regret the experience, or the repercussions of what I did as a result of it. But there was a moment when I opened my eyes and said, "This is not me." In retrospect, I know that this process distanced me from my feminine essence, the caring essence, the emotional essence.

During my spiritual studies, I met many teachers and learned what I could from them. But I always continued onwards, searching. I tried to understand how to put into practice everything I had learned, how to empower and strengthen myself spiritually. But I felt like I had my fill. I felt like a car that enters a garage for cleaning and is dirty again a week later. I felt that the process was endless, that something was wrong with it, that I must reach the point where I am not dependent on a teacher, that I am not dependent on anyone else, that I have independent tools for internal observation and the possibility of doing my own cleansing and release. What do I mean by cleansing and release? Life and spiritual work teach us lessons, and each lesson we learn cleans us from the layers, from the scars that we collect during the course of our lives. These can be lessons in self-confidence, in self-esteem, in patience, in tolerance, in mercy, in love, in forgiveness, in countless things that we need to work on. But then, after we have learned the lesson, we must look within ourselves and know it on all levels: emotional, rational, spiritual, and conscious. Only when we accept the lesson at all of these levels can the true cleansing take place.

In one of the messages I received, it was made clear to me that I would have one more teacher and then reach the completion. And soon afterwards, I was introduced to the Ahava Raba (Great Love) method and met its founder. Ahava Raba is an energy awareness therapy method combining a symbolic language for unveiling the unconscious and a collection of practical energy tools. At first, I was treated by the founder, and later I was treated by his spouse and partner. For me, their method became a real shortcut for reaching the places I wanted to reach—myself, my true connection with myself and with God—and gave me tools to realize the self in an independent way.

After seeing how Ahava Raba had succeeded in leading me to the places I had searched for my entire life, leading me to my essence, leading me to recognize my sensitivity, I decided to continue and study the method and to integrate one of the tools of Ahava Raba—the Language for Practical Awareness—into the Arison Group. For a long time I had searched for a new, cleaner, authentic, and true language, which can connect us to ourselves at the deepest levels of our being. And years ago I wrote, in one of my visions[1], that

---

[1] More on the concept of "vision" can be found in the next chapter.

we need to learn "a new language, a language of the body, the heart, and the soul, which will generate a significant change in society." Indeed, since integrating the Language for Practical Awareness into the Arison Group, I have witnessed significant changes in myself and in those around me. The language of Ahava Raba is a conscious language that facilitates honest communication and provides tools for fulfillment and for realizing personal and group potential. It is a therapeutic language and a symbolic one, whose purpose is to bring the consciousness to the surface, and thus enhance awareness.

Today, after working with the method, I feel I have reached the end of my search. Today, I engage in studies because they enrich me. I try new things because they arouse my curiosity. But I am no longer in a state of spiritual exploration. I am in a state of spiritual connection.

When I was about twelve years old, I read Hermann Hesse's book *Siddhartha*, and it made a profound impact on me. I understood that it is possible to search throughout our entire lifetime, to wander far and wide, to seclude ourselves, to study, to meet one teacher after another, and to finally come to realize that all of the answers are found within us. This lesson embedded itself in me, and it is only today, years after reading the book and after experiencing so much, that I understand how meaningful this message is for my life.

The method we use to learn is not the truth, but the path to truth. Self-learning is important in and of itself. It is the reason why I have never completely adhered or devoted myself to a single and exclusive teaching or method. I believe that something exists beyond the teaching, even beyond the Jewish Torah, even though I am very connected to the Jewish religion and as a Jew feel responsibility to transformation. I am very connected to these messages, and still I feel that there is something above and beyond that links all of the world's teachings.

Each one of us has an essence, and there is a divine spark in the essence of each of us. The most precise image I can suggest is a diamond covered with mud, mud that has solidified and hardened. Until all of the mud is removed, there is no way of knowing that a diamond lies beneath it. Each and every one of us has a diamond within us. The question is how much mud is covering it. There are people with a little bit of mud, and there are some with a lot.

As long as we have not succeeded in cleaning the mud from us, it is what others see. Our mud is what communicates with their mud. In other words, there is no clean communication. We must reach a situation in which it is our essences that communicate with each other.

This "dirty" communication, the lack of true, essential communication, is the basic reason, in my view, for the difficult situation of the world today. But a person cannot work on his communication with another person before he knows himself, his own essence. The awareness of the essence is what enables us to see where the mud is coming from, and where our impulses originate. If I say something to someone in anger or shout at him, I may forget the entire incident after a few minutes and continue on with my life. This is how most of the world operates. But what most of the world fails to understand is that this anger, this energy, does not disappear. It poisons our internal and external environment in the same way that the toxic materials we use pollute our physical environment. The shouting, the insult, and the anger become more intense, and create hatred and evil. When this is what we bring to the world, this is the shape the world takes. We must stop and examine ourselves and try to understand: Why did I shout? Why did I become angry? Where is this coming from? As we examine ourselves in greater depth, we discover more and more layers, more and more shells. And when we learn to know them, we will also be able to release them and be liberated from them— until we reach the root of our pure essence.

Each of us must choose the best way to reach and know his essence. For each person, a different way is true. There is one truth, but many ways of reaching it. The problem is that it is easier for people to believe that if there is one truth, then there is only one path. It seems more orderly to them. They do not have to choose between possibilities. Over the course of the years, I have discovered that the same pattern of thinking also appears in the business world. People do not want to think on their own. They are ready to work and will work hard, from morning till night, investing all they have in it, neglecting their children, family, and everything else for the business, but they do not want to think. They want to be told what to do.

The moment we begin to pose questions to people and begin to challenge them and to demand that they delve more deeply to understand something within themselves, their confidence is undermined, and their whole world is shaken. I see this over and over again because in my business I demand that people open their eyes, open their minds, think beyond, look ahead, and change. And I experience and see the resistance.

I have always met this resistance, at all levels: at the personal level, the interpersonal level, the family level, the business level, the social level, the community level, even at the national level, as I experienced when I left Israel a few years ago. And in the face of all this resistance, only faith and spirituality have strengthened me. I knew that if I encountered so much resistance, I must be on the right path. Following the path of my belief is what has strengthened me. Without it, I would have collapsed. But I simply knew that I was trying to bring to the world something new, different, clean, and good, and that it was difficult for people to accept change.

I learned to see a lesson in resistance, and not only in resistance but in every test or trial that life had placed on my path. In interpersonal relations, in business challenges, in constitutional matters, in everything. I examine everything I encounter as a reflection of something within me: If I am not understood, what am I failing to explain? If I am resisted, what am I failing to convey? What is this experience teaching me about myself?

During long periods in my life, through many crises, I have endured great frustration. I could not understand why people do not see me, do not see the truth. These people could be those around me, media people, or people in any other relationship. They are blind, I thought. But that was my lesson. Their blindness reflected something in me. At one time, I believed that my lesson was to become stronger and grow, but the attempt to do this only hardens the layers. Today I know that if the world around me is not authentic, this is primarily due to the fact that I am not being authentic myself. And today my whole being is devoted to reaching this authenticity, to reaching my essence.

For several decades now, I have been searching for the essence, on a journey to understand it, and I am learning to recognize more each and every day. In recent years, I have experienced a great revelation regarding my sensitivity and its role in my life. I have always been very sensitive to my surroundings, but it is only recently that I have learned to be sensitive to myself. Previously, I could always come and say: "I'm hurt, I'm angry," although it took me many years to reach a true understanding of my feelings. Today, however, I understand that I experience things first of all via the emotions, that I myself am entirely "emotion." So, when I am agitated or hurt, I know that this is my natural response and that I should not blame others for my feelings. It does not belong to them; it belongs to my experience. This is the way in which I decipher the world.

As I have already stated, in order to reach the essence, the diamond within, we must clean the mud off, take off the shells, the wrappings, the layers of protection we accumulated throughout our lives, the defenses we created to protect our essence from injury. As a Jew, I believe that our soul is pure. We come from God. We are a part of God. Thus, we come from purity. From the moment we are born, when our soul enters the human body, we set off and accumulate layer upon layer. We create these shells to protect ourselves from insult, injury, anger, guilt, insecurity, low self-esteem, jealousy. To protect ourselves from all of the painful feelings that leave their mark on us, from everything that we do not want to feel. The problem is that these shells do not disappear. They become part of us, pushing us further and further from our true essence, from ourselves. We lose ourselves. We are wrapped in so many layers that our contacts with our surroundings are not pure, are not true. They take place via the shells, the layers—and not through our essences. Only when we begin to do inner consciousness work and look inside, at ourselves—only then is it possible to say: Here I was hurt, here I got angry, here I did not forgive. Only after seeing the shells is it possible to let go, and this release strips away the layers. This process is endless because if we were perfect we would not be here. But as we strip away more and more layers, we come closer to the authentic essence. The purity. Each layer that is stripped away exposes much sadness, much anger, much insult. The process is not easy, and for most people, unconsciously, there is great resistance. People will use cynicism, hatred, disdain, or scorn to dismiss the need for real inner consciousness work, to avoid looking into themselves. In the past, I never understood where this resistance came from. After all, who would not want to be purer? Cleaner? Who would not want to uncover the diamond within? But today I understand. Today I know that the closer we come to the essence, the more difficult the path becomes. The lessons become harder as we advance. The closer we come to our essence, the stronger the temptation will be to stop, to deviate from the path.

There is a war of light against darkness raging within us. The war that we see in the world around us is a reflection of the battle that is occurring within us. It emanates from this internal battle. Once we try to accept ourselves, for example, to respect ourselves, an internal voice will come and try to undermine our confidence, shake our faith. Suddenly, something will put us to the test: Will we continue to walk along the straight, good, true, and authentic path, or will we be dragged down?

Despite all of my self-work, I have strayed toward anger, frustration, sadness, and affront—more than just once or twice.

In my decades of seeking inner peace, I have become increasingly aware of the fierce battle raging within me— between sadness and happiness, between acceptance and frustration, between praise and envy, between strength and lack of confidence, between the adult and the child. I have recognized the evil inclination within me. The dark side. The closer we get to our inner essence, to the divine spark that resides in every human being, the closer we get to the basis of the evil within us. Just as I saw God within me, the Garden of Eden within me, so I saw Satan and hell within me. This can be a harrowing experience; it is exceedingly difficult to accept that we have within us something that is evil. Acknowledging this can be painful, but to be able to choose the good, to opt for life, we must reach this place.

When I would tell people that happiness, tranquility, and peace are not connected to anything external but flow from within, they would always respond: "Ah, that's easy enough for you to say. You've got money, you've got a yacht, you've got a plane." No one understood that none of this is connected to anything. On the contrary.

For a long time, I was tormented by possessions like my yacht or my private jet, things that are supposed to bring me pleasure, but which I never truly enjoyed. I possess these things for reasons that are external to me: for my children, for my husband, for the status, for entertaining guests. But I suffer from the fact that they are in my possession. From an ecological perspective, from the standpoint of sustainability, I feel that it simply isn't right to own these things; they are too flashy, too extravagant, too wasteful. In short, they are not consistent with my values. Not that I have anything against private jets or yachts as a matter of principle. There is nothing wrong with being content with what you have, and if this is what you have—that's terrific. But I was never able to be happy about material things. In fact, just the opposite is true. For years, I debated whether or not to sell certain items like the yacht and the jet, and when the global economic crisis hit, I felt, among many other things, a certain sense of relief. It provided me with the perfect excuse to put them up for sale, in addition to sharpening my understanding that we do not have to consume more than we really need. I saw that many people, myself included, had lost a sense of proportion, behaving as if there is no end to material desire without being fully aware of the consequences of this excessive consumption upon their soul, and upon the world.

I've always thanked God for the many gifts I have received, and I've never taken material things too seriously, because I know that what's here today will not necessarily be here tomorrow. I realize that whatever happens to me, I will see it as a part of my mission, my path, something that had to occur, a lesson. We cannot take money to the grave; we can take only our values with us to the world beyond. This is the only "commodity" the soul accumulates.

During most of my life, I have been very sad and very frustrated, and all the money in the world could not have helped me get rid of those negative feelings. Because just as the good begins and ends within me, so does the bad. I could be on a dream vacation—blue skies and sunshine, parties galore, crystal-clear water, plus quiet and tranquility—and within a split second, I could be in hell, despite having the best room and the best food and the best of everything. Because hell or heaven is within, and each of us can choose in which of them we wish to spend our lives.

My process of self-acceptance began in earnest when I learned to look upon my sensitivity to the world as a gift rather than a burden, and when I understood that I must find and nurture greater sensitivity for myself. Acceptance can come only after reaching and internalizing this understanding; it is impossible to live in true abundance and freedom when self-acceptance is lacking. One of the most difficult things for me to accept in myself was the fact that I am extremely attentive to details. Each and every detail. To the point of excess. This has made things very hard both on myself and on those around me, because even if there are nine perfect things and one that is not, I will immediately focus on the one that is not. I see all the good things, of course, but I also inevitably notice what's not good enough. People around me sometimes feel as if I'm constantly judging them, constantly demanding. They often fail to see that I am, first and foremost, demanding of myself, that I am my own harshest judge.

The fact that people did not see the details I saw and failed to pay attention to them would hurt me personally: if something I requested was not carried out down to the last detail as I knew it should be done, I took it as a personal affront. I would wonder: Was I not clear enough? I felt as if I gave my all to the people around me—give, give, give— and what did I get in return? This isn't right, and that's not right, and that's not right either. I was constantly frustrated, and the people around me were frustrated too, because no matter what I did, it was never enough. I was never satisfied and neither was anyone else. Today, now that I understand my essence, I realize that I don't have to use my ability to notice details for the purpose of judging and making demands. I learned that I pick up on each and every detail, and that there are billions of details in this world—the whole of humanity. My lesson is to accept most of the details as they are and to focus only on those that I am able to change. This lesson was a revelation for me. Today, I am setting out on a new path. I want to live with eyes wide open, to go on seeing all the many details, but to learn to accept them, to learn to focus on my authentic will, on what is consistent with my purpose.

I learned another important lesson during the long and difficult years in which I was engaged in legal battles in Israel and in the United States, fighting accusations that were totally baseless. During these years, I was often present in the courtroom, and I felt like I was watching actors on a stage. A play. Some judges who think they are God, lawyers from one side against lawyers from the other side. And I, who believe that God is the only supreme judge, would sit and watch this play, in Miami and in Israel, knowing that it bore no connection whatsoever to the truth. How did I cope with this? I've often told myself that difficult experiences are lessons whose purpose is to strengthen and empower me. For a long time, I sincerely believed that life lessons, by their very nature, had to be difficult.

Then I learned to see that this perception, too, is a shell. There are many spiritual concepts in which you can get stuck, playing a game with yourself, a game that is detached from the true inner self while still using spiritual tools and a spiritual language. And since I had assembled a wealth of spiritual tools and concepts, I could fool myself. All this time, I continued to engage in spiritual work, and all this time, I was actually feeding myself fairy tales. I was completely disconnected from what my body experienced. I did not allow myself to feel what was inside of me. Of course, during this period I got angry, I wept, I was sad and hurt, but all of these feelings remained superficial, emanating from the shell. I did not allow myself to feel them deeply, in my essence and in my body. And then I discovered that the body remembers everything—the time we spent in our mother's womb, our birth, our previous incarnations. The body never forgets. Everything is nestled there within us. I believe this is one of the primary reasons we become ill; when the body, weakened and tired, can no longer bear this burden, all the difficulties we have accumulated in our lives erupt as an illness.

Through the process in which I'm engaged today, I also release things from within my body, because all the shells that we cleanse from our souls must subsequently be cleansed from our bodies. And I'm certain that if I did not perform this cleansing, I would find myself very ill in a few years' time. Two methods I have recently tried have helped me greatly in cleansing away what's left of the shells: craniosacral therapy—a method that treats the physical body in order to release it from traumas and experiences that remain in the tissues long after they occurred; and family constellations—a method that does not necessarily focus on the body, but enabled me to release from myself things that were passed on to me from previous generations, such as family or national traumas, which become part of our emotional and physical DNA.

When you cleanse yourself of the shells, you find your true and authentic will, the will of the soul. This discovery changes many things, and it sometimes happens that the people around us may no longer be right for us. Perhaps they suited us in the past because they suited our shells, but they are no longer right for our essence. As the will grows stronger, we are forced to make choices that are increasingly difficult. But there is no alternative. We must respect the other and send him on his way, with love. We must not remain with people who are better suited to our old shells, and this applies to all levels—personal, interpersonal, or business. The only level on which discovery of will cannot lead to such change is between parents and children, because this is a place of unconditional love.

When I spoke at the Israeli Parliament (Knesset) in honor of International Women's Day, I had an opportunity to address the subject of the connection between parents and children, as well as other important topics:

Speech at the Knesset in Honor of International Women's Day, 2009

Allow me to begin with a confession: I have never identified with women's organizations—neither in theory nor in practice. I have always claimed— and I still claim—that I am not in favor of women; I am in favor of human beings. I believe in balance. I believe that balancing between feminine work and masculine work is the correct combination. Men have certain capabilities and women have other capabilities. The two complement each other.

In my group, the Arison Group, which is a philanthropic business group, I have promoted many women, but not due to a feminist agenda. I did not promote women because they are women. I promoted women who were worthy of promotion, women with capabilities, women who worked hard, intelligent women, women with loyalty and intuition—each of them contributing know-how and skills that enhance the system.

Many people believe that I grew up with a silver spoon in my mouth, but the opposite is true. I began working at a fast food restaurant in Miami at age thirteen to earn my allowance, and I have not stopped working since, working hard, primarily in a male setting. This was always my natural setting.

I think the time has come that we, women, stop accusing. We should stop accusing the other, but first of all we should stop accusing ourselves. The time has come to stop being victims, to stop trying to satisfy the other, and to start to become stronger.

I would like to emphasize that there is a difference between force and power—force comes from an aggressive place, a place where women fight for their place in a masculine world. Feminine strength, on the other hand, stems from inside, from the deepest and most basic place in every woman: the intuition, the ability to see a broad picture, the caring, the softness.

I have received a great gift in my life—and no, it is not the gift you are surely thinking of. My great gift is my children, the gift of motherhood. I think that motherhood, more than anything else, teaches unconditional love, love that does not depend on anything, because whatever our children do—we love them. This natural maternity is found in every woman, even if she has no children, and we can and must bring this love to our places of work, and to the world.

So how do we reach strength, advancement, key positions?

I know that not all women have financial resources, but I also know that the first rule is will—the will to learn, the will to grow stronger, the will for empowerment, the will to advance and grow. I believe that each woman must first of all know herself. Self-knowledge is a process that entails removing all of the masks we put on ourselves during our lives, in order to reach the inner truth—the essence.

This perhaps sounds like a simple task, but the truth is that this is the most difficult task.

We invest our entire lives in this mission, whether or not we are aware of it, and we do not always succeed in fulfilling it.

The reason for this is that our true self, our essence, is hidden behind many layers of defense, which influence all of us in different and unseen ways, generating insult, hurt, pressure, fear, and more.

These layers, which accumulate within us from childhood and throughout the course of our lives, are layers we must remove in order to reach the inner essence and self-change.

In order to respect—we must respect ourselves. In order to love—we must love ourselves. In order to attain peace—we must reach peace with ourselves.

The key is to maintain the proper harmony between our inner self and our thoughts, words, and actions. We can sometimes smile at someone, but at the same time kill him with the feeling we are emanating. When the words and the actions contradict each other—we will not be able to touch our inner strength and transmit it externally.

The first rule, therefore, is consciousness. The second rule, which complements it, is know-how—knowledge in the field in which you seek to work. I believe that the combination of consciousness and knowledge is what produces the best result. The path can be complicated, even difficult, because there are always external factors that try to drag us down, to keep us small, but ultimately we must take responsibility for ourselves and for our future.

Every woman can, and this does not depend only on the resources at her disposal. If there are no

financial means, it is possible to learn via the Internet, from books, or with the help of a friend, but we need to remember that no one will help us, or even think to help, if we do not know how to ask or receive. That is a lesson in itself.

I believe that everything is in our hands. We only need to want to know, and to understand, and then to assume responsibility and set out on our way. And most important of all: not to let anyone pull us down. Because with the correct combination of consciousness and knowledge, the world is open to each and every one of us.

Today I know that what I want to include in my life relates first of all to my personal realm, to my mission to lead to a new world, to my future, to my connection with God, with the universe, with my authentic will, with my personal relationships.

If each one of us, as an individual, would engage in inner consciousness work and look inward, a change would begin. But this change is only the beginning, because after the personal, internal work, the interpersonal work begins. We need to learn a new language that will enable us to communicate on a different level, to engage in consciousness work with each other, to see that our shells clash with each other. And then we will no longer be able to dismiss the other, to be angry at him, to hurt him, to cause him pain, to cast the responsibility on him, because the moment there is consciousness, the first thing each of us does is to look inward, to understand: Where is the anger coming from? What is the source within me of the insult that I try to hurl at the other? How is it connected to him, and how is it connected to me?

This is ongoing work; you do not just take a course and that's it. It is a process that accompanies you throughout your entire life, and it is one of the principles that everyone who works with me understands, desires, and chooses. All of us do consciousness work on a daily basis. This includes me and all of the people around me, in all circles of relationships—from the personal to the business. The impact of this work is also circular, spreading like ripples in water.

After years in which I facilitated, suggested, invited—I no longer hide behind anything. This is one of the requirements for anyone who wishes to work in my group. I seek a new world. A different one. A new world does not start on the outside. It starts here. Just as for me it starts within, it also starts within for everyone. And therefore, if I want to bring something different to the world, it must start first of all in my group. But also in this effort, as in many places in my life, I have encountered resistance—not on the part of the people closest to me, who are connected to themselves and engage in inner consciousness work routinely. When I explained to them that this is the path I wish to lead, they willingly followed. But there were people who felt coercion, and it was clear to me that I was not interested in imposing anything on anyone. Each of us chooses his life, chooses what he wants it to be. Naturally, these choices have ramifications that should be taken into consideration. In the pre-computer era, the requirements for a secretary included using a typewriter and sometimes taking shorthand. Today, in the era of computers, everyone, whether a secretary or a manager, must know how to use them. No one would employ a secretary who does not know how to use a computer. It is a basic requirement. In my view, in the new era that I am trying to create, in the new world for which I am preparing myself, consciousness work is a basic requirement. Therefore, I demand that all of my employees engage in it. This is not coercion, but choice. Anyone who is interested in working for me, with me, to be part of my vision, must meet this basic requirement—must know how to use his internal computer.

In my view, this is an immense transformation in my internal feeling, in my strength, in my growth, in my vision, and in my communication, as well as in my interpersonal relations—in everything. There were many people who thought that I was hallucinating, dreaming, mad. They pretended that they understood me, but behind my back there was much gossip, scorn, and cynicism. But thanks to my sensitivity, it was very easy to see beyond these masks. If you smile at someone, and your body is emitting hatred or anger, it is quite transparent. The entire world is becoming more and more transparent, and it is impossible to say one thing and echo something else. This no longer works. I saw, knew, and felt, but did not always act. I simply continued onward and said to myself that things will work out in time.

But I did not encounter only resistance. I also received a lot of encouragement, support, and love. And with time, most of my employees, even those who resisted at first, began to see that they are capable of leading other people and showing them the way as well. They began to see that this inner consciousness work also helps them in their personal lives. They grew and strengthened, and today have a clearer and sharper view—one that is more positive, more believing, and more accepting of the light, the power, and the abundance of life. It is clear that we all endure setbacks, make mistakes, and have arguments. Nothing is perfect, and even someone who does spiritual work with himself can fall apart. But I always collect myself anew and continue on. And the beauty in consciousness is that it allows me to start over each time, to collect myself each time, from a higher place.

Today I know that much of what I once saw as a lack of understanding on the part of people is actually fear. It is much easier to say, "I don't understand what you want," than, "Yes, I understand, but I'm afraid to try." I know that the resistance and evil I have encountered stem from a fear of the new.

When one wishes to bring forth something new into the world, something that is not understood, something that is ahead of its time—it is frightening. It is threatening, and this fear creates evil in certain people, leading them to try to suppress the new because it threatens their sense of belonging. The soul wants to move ahead, but the body wants to survive, not to budge, to hang on, and therefore people do not want to change. This is true at all levels, even at the national level: indeed, all of us in Israel are real survivors. We have undergone wars and terror attacks; we are all strong, the children are strong, the parents are strong. We all hang onto our strength and do not really look inside to see how deep the wound is because such introspection frightens us—what if the things we discover within require us to make a change? It is much easier to resist, to repress, and even to try to kill off the new and different rather than to open the heart and accept, to contend with the new. It is much more comfortable for people to remain with the "old."

This hanging-on comes from the ego. When someone keeps saying all the time, "mine, mine, mine," he probably thinks it is not his. Because if something really belongs to us, and we know it to be true, we do not need to say this or fight for it. In Israel, when we say that we are fighting for our existence, we are actually saying that we are feeling insecure, that everything we have could be taken from us in a moment. If we believed with complete faith that we have the right to be here, that God is protecting us, and that nothing can change this, we would not need to fight so much. It is true that many in the Arab world do not want the State of Israel to exist. That is a fact. They are militant and belligerent; that is a fact. The question is what we choose to do with these facts. The solution is not to wage war against those who oppose us, nor to extend a hand of friendship to those who attempt to wage war against us. The solution is to recognize the boundaries that exist between us and to respect them, on the one hand, while, on the other hand, to bolster our faith in ourselves, in our strength, in our ability to liberate the Palestinians from their dependency on us, and move onward. We must not perpetuate this dependency because it creates feelings of inferiority, hatred, and weakness, and constitutes one of the greatest obstacles facing us and our neighbors in achieving true peace. Dependency does not allow a person real freedom. It does not enable a person to realize his potential. It binds him, limits him, weakens him. The State of Israel must find the way to stop giving the Palestinians the things that perpetuate their dependency—money, water, electricity—and to start providing tools that allow them to stand on their own feet. These tools will also cost money, but investment in independence is something completely different than investment in dependency. Fishing poles also cost money, but they are immeasurably more important than fish. Of course, the Palestinians might oppose this type of process. Someone who has become accustomed to dependency will be reluctant to give it up. Dependency is addictive, but we must understand that we have no control over the way in which they decide to react. We can only control ourselves in the way we treat them, and separate ourselves from them in the best way possible. At the same time, we must defend our borders, and invest the effort and funds that are currently used to maintain our mutual dependency in protecting what is ours: the security of our borders, our land, our air and sea, our weapons of defense, our intelligence-gathering. We must be powerful, but not forceful, and we must bolster our faith in ourselves because borders alone are not enough. We must believe in and change ourselves if we want to bring change to the Middle East. In a message I recently received, I saw the State of Israel from a bird's-eye view and was told that borders alone will not change the situation in the region. Only our energy will bring true change.

It is important for me to emphasize that I am not saying this from any political point of view. I am neither a left-winger nor a right-winger, and I have no intention of entering the political arena. I analyze the political situation according to the insights I have derived from other spheres of life, from the personal to the business, insights that are true in relation to all levels of existence.

It is important that we do not act from a place of ego, of insecurity and lack of faith, but instead from our essence. And I believe that our essence, that of the Jewish people, is to bring about *tikkun olam*, to transform the world.

We must break our old patterns because they no longer work. We must stop returning to the same wrong places, again and again. On the personal, business, and national levels too. People also need to examine themselves in business, to make sure that they are acting out of purity, cleanliness, and honesty. There are many businesspeople who believe that this is the way it works—that manipulation has and always will be part of the world, that there is competition, and that if they do not behave in this way, others will overtake them, and will defeat them. In my eyes, this belief also comes from fear, from something lacking.

I believe that I have received a platform from God, a large and powerful business platform that enables me to bring about change, that enables me to reach people in both the business world and the spiritual world, and to provide them with a role model—to show them that true leadership is a leadership of each and every one of us, and that every one of us can become a leader of his own world, to show that the material and spiritual can come together, that it depends only on each and every one of us. In each of us there is a divine spark and an evil inclination. Both exist within us, and our mission in this world is to recognize, experience, and reach both the spark and this inclination, to look at them with open eyes and to choose the good, not the fear. This should be our mission in our personal life, in business life, in political and diplomatic life. Herein lies the future of our world, of the planet Earth. Herein lies redemption.

Matter

I GREW UP IN A BUSINESS-ORIENTED HOME, IN BOTH AMERICA AND ISRAEL. I ate, drank, and soaked up business all the time. It was part of the air around me. I grew up in a home that was geared towards success and money. It was a home where there was great vision, but no room for emotional development. As I have already explained, I had to find this path on my own.

When I was eight years old, my family moved from New York to Miami, and a year later my parents divorced. While my mother was still finalizing the details of the divorce, I moved to Israel on my own and lived for six months with my uncle and cousin until my mother joined me. I lived in Israel until I was twelve, and after my bat mitzvah I returned to Miami and lived there until I was seventeen. During all those years, I traveled back and forth between Israel and the United States, all of the time. I had friends here and there—in both worlds.

Despite the fact that I only had one more semester before graduating from high school, I decided to come back to Israel, take my matriculation exams, and enlist in the army. This move was very important to me because I felt that life was more meaningful in Israel. When I left the army, I traveled to Miami, thinking that I was coming for a vacation—to go out and have a good time, enjoy myself, and then come back to Israel—but I did not have the money to return, and my father refused to pay for the ticket. I had already worked at a fast food restaurant at age thirteen to earn my allowance, so I knew that I would have to make do on my own. Therefore, I immediately started to work. But then I met my future husband, got married, had children, and found myself staying in Miami for the next sixteen years of my life.

I worked as a travel agent for Carnival Cruise Lines (CCL), the family company, and I really loved my work. I studied at a major airline company and, at the same time, began to learn hotel and restaurant management. But I did not complete my studies. I felt that the teachers did not know what they were talking about, and that the business content I grew up with and was immersed in at home was richer than what I received from my studies. The real school was at home.

I wanted to learn how all of the departments in the company operated, so I worked in reservations, ticketing, sales, and as a buyer for a chain of onboard stores that were still owned by Carnival at the time.

When I no longer wanted to work in the family business, I left and began to work at a very large agency in Miami as a travel agent for local businesspeople.

When my children were born, I left work because it was important for me to devote myself to raising them. But after eight years of full-time motherhood, I began to feel a strong desire and obligation to participate in my family's businesses, which was amplified because, for the first time in my life, I began to receive money from my trust fund. I asked my father to appoint me to the board of directors of the company he had founded, Carnival Cruise Lines, and to offer me a significant position. His offer completely surprised me—he wanted me to establish a philanthropic foundation for the family. He told me that he had received many requests from groups and individuals who wanted him to donate to the Jewish community and to Israel. My father wanted very much to give back to the community in which he lived and worked, and of course to the State of Israel, but did not know how to handle the many requests he received. He had established the National Foundation for Advancement in the Arts (NFAA) and the New World Symphony in Miami, and contributed to various causes, such as the Conservatory of Music and the Arison Garden in Israel. But he felt that someone needed to manage this donation mechanism in an efficient and organized way, and offered this job to me. I had never dreamed of managing a philanthropic foundation, and I had no prior experience or know-how. I was not familiar with this field because I had always believed that my vocation lay in business or in psychology. But I immediately accepted the challenge, and in return my father appointed me to the board of directors, as I had requested. This was the beginning of my path to the boardrooms of large public companies.

I began to build the foundation from scratch. It was clear to me that there was no reason not to manage a philanthropic foundation according to the same standards that applied to regular businesses. Therefore, I researched and examined the large philanthropic organizations in Miami. But in addition to what I learned from them, I used the business knowledge I grew up with and my intuition to build the Arison Foundation (established in the 1980s) and to set the highest standards for it. During those years, fundraising was mainly conducted at magnificent gala evenings in which money was donated to the organization by paying for a place at a table. These gala evenings filled my life. I found myself attending four or five such events a week. In addition, there were cocktail parties, lunches, dinners, and much more. This type of life suits some people, and some think it is wonderful, but I was living a fantasy life that did not connect in any way to my true nature. The dazzling lights, the evening dresses, the public speaking—all of these were alien and very difficult for me. During this period, I was very shy, very introverted. If I was in a room with ten other people, and each person only had to introduce himself, I would feel my heart pounding until it was my turn, just because I needed to say my name. I did not know how my voice sounded; I could not vocalize it. In addition, I was always shadowed by the feeling that everyone wanted something from me, and I did not know why I was the one to decide who would receive help and who would not. These years were not at all simple for me. I felt that everyone was biting off pieces from me. The only moments I felt completely connected were when I was in the midst of the work itself: when I was sitting with the board of directors of Carnival and of other organizations that worked for Israel, the Jewish community, or other educational, cultural, and philanthropic institutions. Only then, I felt that I was in my own territory.

On the eve of the 1991 Gulf War, I had the feeling that something bad was about to happen, that war was about to break out. Even before the war erupted, I saw the missiles falling in my mind's eye. I felt terrified, helpless, and frustrated. And these feelings intensified when the war finally broke out, of course. On the one hand, my country was in danger, my mother, uncles and aunts, cousins, good friends, all were under fire, and I wanted to be there with them. But on the other hand, I did not want to bring my children, who were still young, into this type of situation. Ostensibly, everything continued as usual and life went on, but for me everything happened in slow motion. My body was in Miami, but my heart was in Israel. At that moment, I decided: I am not prepared to feel so torn, and I must return to Israel. And that is what I did. There are many who think that I came to Israel because of my late father, who also decided during the same period to move to Israel with his wife, Lin. The truth is that neither of us knew about the other's decision.

In Israel, I decided that I would not continue to attend galas, lunches, and cocktail parties, and that I would not contribute to things that were of no interest to me. Another decision I made was to separate the Arison Foundation from the Carnival Foundation (which supports a variety of charitable and arts-related organizations) and to transfer the latter's management to someone else. I wanted to manage the Arison Foundation separately—in Israel and for the benefit of Israel.

This period was not easy. I had to start over in a country whose mentality was more dissimilar than I had imagined. I began to operate the foundation on a small scale, but when I started to contribute, I encountered responses that surprised me. I was used to American etiquette, which decreed that you receive a thank-you letter for even the smallest contribution. It was hard for me to adjust to the Israeli character, which sometimes made me feel that everyone was complaining to me and that I was not giving enough. But I have always been a Zionist, and Israel is very important to me, so I continued on, anchoring my roots there deeper and deeper. I started to study psychology, as noted earlier, and art too—mainly painting and sculpture at the Open University and in private classes.

For two years, I toured the country to understand the needs of the community before officially launching the foundation. And then I decided that it would be best to start the foundation's work in Israel with major projects, one or two a year, to devote my all to them and then move on to the next one. I proposed this plan of action to my father, who supported me and asked only that the first major project be the building of the new center for brain research at the Weizmann Institute of Science in Rehovot, one of the most prestigious academic institutes in the country. And so it was.

During that time, the foundation had an external board of directors, and one of its members suggested that I examine the appalling conditions at Tel Aviv Sourasky Medical Center, the largest hospital in Tel Aviv. I went for a visit that made a strong impact on me. I wept uncontrollably when I saw the patients that had to be placed in the corridors because the facilities were overcrowded and insufficient. Since I myself had undergone a very difficult personal experience in a hospital in Israel during one of my vacations, I decided that the first major project I would initiate would involve a hospital. But when I proposed the idea to my father, he did not like it. He said that he preferred to contribute to beautiful things, to the arts, or to gardens. I had to argue with him and ask him to trust me and let me lead the project, despite his reservations. He consented and, together with the hospital director and in accordance with the needs of the physicians and nurses, we began to design a new building for the hospital. We planned every detail, from the architects to the curtains. I put my heart and soul into the project. At the end of my father's life, when he was very ill and had to spend a lot of time in that same hospital, he changed his mind. He came to understand the reasons why I had wanted to contribute to the hospital and admitted to me that it had been a very wise move on my part. I do not know whether he would have wanted to see his name on the building, because my father was a very modest man, but I felt that I must give him this honor and recognition and the Ted Arison Medical Tower was opened in 2001. The Arison Campus for the Arts, the Arison School for Business Administration at the Interdisciplinary Center in Herzliya, and other projects followed. Each of them was a flagship project that I could look at with pride and know that I had made a significant contribution in the fields of research, healthcare, education, and the arts.

At this stage in the foundation's development, I asked the board of directors that we allow the foundation to make smaller donations, because a relatively small sum could also be of great help to a student seeking a scholarship. I met strong resistance. They argued with me, claiming that this would be a headache, that it would require considerable manpower, would be a waste of the foundation's resources, and more. But I held my ground, and we agreed that I would get a one-year trial period. A year later, it was clear that this trial was a success. We contributed to all fields, to various and diverse organizations, and to a great number of people, for communities in need, for children and teenagers in distress, for the arts and culture, sports, healthcare, the disabled, education, and scholarships. We also continued to contribute to major projects, and I received the appreciation and consent of those who had initially opposed this move.

Shari Arison

The Foundation's Vision

The Arison Foundation— A Global Jewish Foundation

OUR CALLING: To transform the Jewish world and thereby set an example for all humanity.

OUR MISSION: To invest in upgrading the quality of life and transforming the human environment.

OUR VISION: Taking responsibility to set an example for a better human environment through basic human values.

OUR CORE VALUES: Our philanthropy is based upon three core Jewish values:

Tzedakah: charity and responsibility
Tikkun Olam: transforming the world
Chessed: acts of loving-kindness

OUR STRATEGIC DESIGN: We believe in philanthropy...

- That listens to everyone and is responsive in offering solutions to a broad spectrum of community needs.
- That supports public infrastructure development leading to the creation of health, educational, and cultural projects that are committed to standards of excellence.
- That creates, cultivates, and nurtures programs that in turn inspire acts of human kindness and tolerance.
- That builds a culture of giving and participation.
- That is both responsive and proactive: responsive in community development grant-making worldwide; proactive in generating original program ideas and partnerships for implementation in Israel and adapting/replicating successful models locally and globally.

We are committed to upgrading the quality of Jewish life in Israel and in Jewish communities throughout the world.

While working to strengthen the Arison foundation, a private enterprise whose contributions are drawn solely from the family's funds, it was important for me also to conduct independent business ventures. Therefore, I acquired the franchise rights for the Mövenpick brand and built roadside restaurants all over Israel. I was involved in every last detail in their planning and construction: in the design, the development of the vision, the wording of the contracts, and the negotiations with the kibbutzim (collective settlements) on whose land the restaurants were built. I did not receive the money to build the restaurants from my father. He wanted me to undertake this endeavor on my own and to assume the responsibility so that I could appreciate the difficulties and risks associated with establishing a business. He told me to take out loans and cope with the burden by myself. I was very surprised by his refusal to invest in my business, but I did not allow this to stop me, and Mövenpick became a big success in Israel. At the same time, I founded the Matan—Your Way to Give organization as a company that raises public funds from corporations and their employees. Matan was based on the model of the American United Way, and its goal was to mobilize the business community for the culture of giving.

I started it in the wake of an ongoing discussion in Israel on the question "Who is a Jew?" Knowing the American mentality, it was clear to me that this topic and the subject of assimilation are leading the Jewish communities in the United States to contribute less to Israel than before and to divert their resources to their own communities. I knew that many people in Israel were worried about the dwindling flow of donations from abroad, but I believed that while we had needed donations from Diaspora Jewry in Israel's early years to survive and establish the state, today this dependency causes us to feel like children in need of the support and guidance of their parents. I felt that the State of Israel's economic prosperity and growth had led us to maturity and that we should become independent and also use our resources and what we have achieved to take care of ourselves. Thus, we could still benefit from the welcome donations we received from generous Jews throughout the world, but as partners, not as needy recipients. The Matan organization was the pioneer and leader in this new path of independence, encouraging involvement and giving by businesses to benefit the community in which they exist, operate, and profit—by both the management and the employees. I am proud to say that Matan changed the culture of business philanthropy in the State of Israel, and today I believe that there is no serious business organization or businessperson who does not contribute to their community. Matan showed both management and employees how to give back to the community through free choice and mobilization, not through coercion. Matan was also meticulous about the level of professional management of the nonprofit organizations with which it worked. It asked to review financial statements, a structured budget, vision, strategy, objectives, and objectives vs. performance. This meticulousness led the organizations to improve and to become more professional.

One of Matan's prominent characteristics—a principle that is very important to me—is that 100% of the funds contributed via the organization reach their destination. I did not want to use the contributions received to finance the operating costs of the organization itself. I wanted to make sure that the donors would be sure that all of their money would go where they wanted it to go.

Therefore, during all of the years in which I was involved in Matan, from 1998 onwards, I myself paid the operating costs. My dream was for Matan to succeed in standing on its own, so that I could release the organization knowing that it would continue to operate—because it is easy when there is one supporter, but it becomes more difficult when it is necessary to find other supporters. I was happy to see this dream fulfilled. Wonderful people took upon themselves the leadership of Matan, contributed money for its operation, and maintained the same policy.

As it is with giving, so it is with tolerance; these two areas have always been very close to my heart, and in addition to my philanthropic activity, I decided to gather a group of people with the goal of creating a short film that would convey a message of tolerance. But unfortunately, and ironically, the members of the group did not stop bickering among themselves. The producer of the film introduced me to someone who understood exactly what I had in mind. We went into the studio, chose the text and characters, edited them, and then I finally had the sought-after film. The film featured friendly animal figures made of clay, each dubbed with a different voice and with various accents and gender in order to portray the widest possible spectrum of groups in Israeli society. The figures said things like: "Our future begins this moment. What time is it?"; "The good in me and the good in you, that's what matters"; "Love is the answer"; "Only if each person plays his instrument music is created. Only by respecting the uniqueness of the other, togetherness is created." This film was broadcast on Israeli television for a year and was intended to serve as the infrastructure for the Department of Children and Teenagers in Essence of Life—an organization that did not yet exist.

While I was still engaged in philanthropic work and my private business development, I tried to fashion for myself a clearer vision of the future. One of the most significant events I experienced in this effort was a meeting with a channeler who told me that my father would bequeath his assets to me. She conveyed many messages to me that, in retrospect, were very precise in regard to the future, and she told me that I was destined to lead the people of Israel. During that period, I did not understand the meaning of this leadership she spoke about, but I knew that I had to clarify my aspirations and my vision for myself, and I turned to a coach who specializes in vision and strategy. At first, the work with him was very difficult. And years later, I learned that there are many who regard him as a controversial figure who stirs considerable opposition. But I found that he helps people think outside the box, beyond themselves, and a million light years into the future, and then helps them to realize how they are about to fulfill what they saw, fulfill their vision. Indeed, there are two ways to look at change: We can look backwards, towards the past, towards the old, and say, "This is what we did during the past year; this year we will do things differently." And the second way is to look forward, towards the future, towards the new, to see what it looks like, how we want it to appear, and then understand how to reach it and which steps will advance us towards it. In this way, it is possible not only to bring about change but a real transformation.

The moment the vision is written and exists and is clear, strategy and tactics can be built to reach it. And the moment that the tactics, strategy, and vision exist, there is a map that enables us to reach the objective and realize the vision.

Vision work means creating the reality that we want to see. A coach cannot do this work for me, because my vision is mine alone. It is part of my soul, part of my view, part of my experience. What the coach can do is to give me the tools to express the vision, visualize it, not only to myself, but to others, to the world. Since then, I have written many visions, and each time my vision expands wider and wider. And each time that I reach a new vision, I feel that I am the leading instrument in an orchestra. My entire body trembles and resonates the moment I hit the right note. The greatness of a true vision is measured by whether it is still the same vision when examined ten years later. There is something in a great vision that does not change, that is always true. The way in which we fulfill it—the strategy, the tactics—all this can change, but the vision remains the same vision.

I tried to prepare myself for a future in my father's businesses, but I found that I had to fight him, to prove to him that I knew what I was doing and what I wanted. This friction between us angered and saddened me very much. I feared that he opposed allowing me to participate in his businesses out of chauvinism, because I am a woman. Today,

I think that he was looking out for me, that he did not want to burden me with the enormous responsibility, the worries and difficulties that accompany the extensive businesses he managed. But at that time, we did not have good communication between us. He simply said, "No, that's the way I want it." And immediately I felt hurt because I assumed that he thought I was not good enough. But I kept on trying. It was bigger than me. I knew that I had a mission and that this was the way to fulfill it.

Finally, when my father acquired Bank Hapoalim, the largest bank in Israel, he changed his mind and appointed me to the board of directors of the bank and of Arison Investments. During my first year on the bank's board of directors, I did not speak. I just listened; I wanted to learn. I realized that I did not understand anything about banking, but the experience I had accrued at Carnival Cruises, working at various levels of the company, helped me a lot. It is true that this was a financial organization and not a cruise line, but I understood, from top to bottom, how an organization works, how it is constructed—from both a systemic perspective and via practical experience. In addition, I had many years of experience as a member of Carnival's board of directors, which gave me a perspective on the way a public company operates. I knew and had an in-depth understanding of what constitutes sound management, and the relevant laws and the responsibility of a board member. In addition to all this, I grew up with a great businessman. I knew what vision is, what strategy is, but I did not sufficiently trust myself at that time. I did not use my intuition. The external voices blurred the internal voices. I did not know who I really was and did not rely on my inner voice. I constantly had to prove to myself, to the world, that I was capable.

When I tried to clarify what the bank's vision was, I was shocked to discover that the only vision was profit. I proposed to the members of the board and the joint owners to participate in developing a new vision for the bank, but I did not receive their cooperation and finally was forced to work on the vision by myself, with my coach. I wanted to facilitate a situation in which the bank respects the client, whoever he may be, because I believe that every client, big or small, is important. But, unfortunately, this was not the attitude at the time. I encountered a lot of resistance to this principle from those who argued that small clients are less important because they generate less profit for the bank. But I felt that this was a wrong approach, and I fought for my views.

Another area in which I invested great effort was in branding the bank. It was simply a subject that disturbed me visually. In those years, you could find three branches of the bank in the same neighborhood, each of which had a separate look, with different signs and logos from three different periods of time. My attempt to explain the importance of uniformity and the power of a brand was also not easy.

I also worked to promote a policy of contributing to the community, through mobilization, of course, and not through coercion, and I brought Matan into the bank. I wanted everyone to understand how important it is in my view to give back to the community in which we live, because we are the community and the community is us, and to understand that giving is more than just a supreme value and obligation. Giving promotes a feeling of camaraderie among the workers and a knowledge that they are working for a place they can be proud of, a worthy place that has important messages and principles.

Today, in my tours of the bank, when I see employees for whom each customer is important, who sit in branches that have a uniform and orderly appearance, who are proud of their giving—I feel great joy.

While still in the United States, I donated a modest sum to a museum in Israel focusing on the settlers that came to the land of Israel in the late nineteenth century. When I moved to Israel, I increased the amount of donations, but the project still did not take off. Finally, my father, who had a special place in his heart for the museum, asked me to take responsibility for completing it. I found myself signing a contract with the local council and dealing with building supervisors, architects, and contractors who did not want to return to the project because of delayed payments and holdups that had lasted for years. But despite these difficulties, the museum opened in 1998. My father was very proud of me, and at the dedication ceremony he turned to me on the stage and said, "It's all thanks to you." It was the first time in my life that he recognized my work in this way, and in public.

It was precisely at the time when my father began to see the fruits of my work that I started to sense that his life was nearing its end. In one of my meditations, I saw my late grandmother (my father's mother) and previous generations of ancestors. They told me that they were waiting for his arrival, and I knew at that moment that his death was approaching. When I described the experience to a healer I met with during that period, he told me that my father would likely live for up to another year, but no more. I understood that I had to prepare myself on all levels: emotional, spiritual, financial, and organizational. Despite the new recognition and appreciation I had won from him, I knew that he did not intend for me to inherit his businesses. But I remembered that years earlier I had met with a channeler who told me that before his death he would change his mind, and I believed that this would indeed occur.

I consulted with the coach who had assisted me with the work on the vision. I tried to understand how I was supposed to design a vision for my future businesses when on the one hand I had the restaurants, the Arison foundation, and positions on boards of directors, while on the other hand there was an empire that I was not supposed to inherit, but which, according to the channelings, I was about to receive and lead. The coach advised me first of all to consult with an attorney, and that is what I did. They prepared for me the documents required for changing the company's bylaws and stock registration, so that I would be ready for the moment everything changes.

In one of my first conversations with the coach, he asked me to look twenty years ahead, into the future. I did not understand what he wanted from me. "Where are you?" he asked me. "What are you doing? How does your life look? How does your business life look?" He gave me a frame in which I could imagine everything I wanted, and I saw that I wanted to bring peace to the world.

Despite the fact that years earlier Dr. Brian Weiss had told me that I was destined to contribute to world peace, and despite the fact that the channeler had told me that I would lead the people of Israel, and despite the fact that my coach had told me that I have the ability to lead, I was still extremely introverted. I tried to understand what my calling was and arrived each time at the same answer: world peace. I told my coach that I am not a prime minister and that I do not intend to be a prime minister, so what is my connection with world peace? How can I contribute to world peace? But then I received a message: to achieve peace in the world, each one of us must achieve peace with himself and his surroundings. Peace begins within ourselves. Other messages followed that helped me to begin to crystallize and write the vision. One night, I woke up after midnight and received another message, long and continuous, which I would later call the "road map" of inner peace.

Essence of Life

Core Values

When we achieve peace with ourselves individually and with our surroundings— together we will reach world peace.

We all are one—but every individual is unique.

We are God's children and everyone has a divine spark.

Everyone has virtues—love, compassion, tranquility, unity, purity, happiness, truth, light, power, knowledge, etc.

There is one source of power.

Unity—we are part of a greater whole. We come into the world as separate entities, where each one has his or her unique destiny and role. Therefore, we should strive to be united.

We all have the right and ability to reach internal happiness and tranquility.

We all have the free choice and the responsibility to influence our lives and create our reality.

Our essence is love.

We are souls and human beings.

The universe provides us with an infinite number of ways and clues how to reach our essence, develop, grow, and get to know ourselves.

One can observe, listen, and know oneself.

The experience of life is, in every given moment, the here and now—the present.

Everything exists simultaneously.

The power of thought creates reality.

The individual reflects and is a reflection of the Other.

Every action has a reaction (the universal law of karma).

The world functions in circularity and is constantly changing (seasons, night and day, birth and death).

We strive to achieve internal balance—body, mind, spirit, and soul—in all the levels of our existence.

We can learn to connect to our own virtues, thus comprehending and connecting to those of other individuals.

We teach and learn simultaneously, in a continuous, infinite process.

Everyone is responsible for strengthening the relations between the individual, the community, and nature.

> We are all in a journey of remembrance whose purpose is to connect us to the essences of our souls and the understanding that all is one.
>
> Constant development and changes in our perceptions and growth bring about the change in our personal and collective awareness.

I understood that I have a calling, that I have a mission, and though it is contrary to my nature as an introvert, in the future I would have to lead. Slowly, I learned to accept and to give thanks for this, and for the fact that I am a woman of vision and that I have foresight. Apparently, this is in my genes. I took this for granted for many years, and today I know that this is my gift. This is a gift that pained me for a long time and frustrated me very much, because it made me feel that I am different, that no one understands me, because I saw things that no one else was able to see. I felt that something was wrong with me. Only after a lot of self-work, I understood that I actually have a gift, a uniqueness, something that many people do not have.

We are each unique in our own way, but we are not the same. We are all part of one large whole. Each of us is a piece in a puzzle. There are pieces of all sizes, shapes, colors, but none of us has the complete picture. Each piece of the puzzle is different and unique. We are all children of God. We are all human beings. We are all part of One, but each of us is different.

Three months before his death, my father was hospitalized in respiratory intensive care. During those months, I handled all of his business affairs behind the scenes. The managers executed their work, but the final decisions were mine. The intensive care room was in the old part of the hospital, underground, without any daylight. My father was given artificial respiration and lost his voice, and during one of my visits he handed me a note on which he wrote with great effort: "You are my heir." Though I was prepared for this possibility, I did not understand at first what he was trying to tell me. I asked him, "Do you want to change everything?" and he nodded. I saw that despite his difficult condition he felt a great relief. When his condition improved a bit, and he was able to sit and talk, I brought all of the paperwork to him, ready for him to sign. After he returned home from the hospital, I asked him if he was sure about the decision he had made. "Very sure," he told me. I explained to him that the businesses in themselves do not interest me, and that I see them as an instrument for changing the State of Israel and the entire world. I shared my thoughts about mission and soul with him, and he listened intently. When I finished, he only said, "I didn't understand a thing, but you are very interesting."

Soon afterwards, my father passed away.

All of the responsibility for managing the Arison assets in Israel fell upon me overnight. In addition, I had to deal with the complicated estate without any assistance except for the earlier preparation I had done. I encountered people who tried to deceive me and many difficulties in the business area, with the family, with myself, while a heavy atmosphere of mourning hovered above everything.

One of my first decisions after my father's death was to change the foundation's name to the Ted Arison Family

Foundation and to part gratefully from the members of its external board of directors, because I understood that it was important for me that the board be composed of foundation employees and not an external body. I wanted each of the foundation's employees to be part of the giving and to understand why we are contributing and what we are doing. The largest projects remained under my supervision, and today they are handled by Jason, my son, who manages the foundation and continues to follow in my footsteps, and I completely support his decisions. Another decision I made after my father's death was to create a special department that helps rehabilitate individuals who turn to the foundation, to provide them with tools for independence and growth. Fishing poles, and not fish. This is a model department, which operates in close collaboration with the Department of Welfare. Its principles and the reasons for its success are studied at universities.

I then had to clarify for myself what I should concentrate on, which of the businesses I inherited I should focus on. I made up my mind, and gradually sold a newspaper, a communication company, and a substantial part of the high-tech and biotech companies owned by Arison Investments.

I also had to decide what to do with the roadside facilities and Mövenpick restaurant chain in Tel Aviv. The troubled political situation in Israel and the frequent terror attacks in the late 1990s left many of the roadside restaurants abandoned. There were no visitors. Despite the fact that the restaurant in Tel Aviv was busy and popular, I decided to minimize the damage and close it and the roadside restaurants, realizing that such businesses require the constant presence of the owners and that I needed to invest all my attention in the bank. That was my greatest responsibility. Before his death, my father asked me to be the chairwoman of the bank, and I refused. "What do I know about it?" I said, and I did not reveal to him that his request scared me to death. His answer has stayed with me to this very day: "You have intuition," he said. "And that is all you need."

During the two years after his death, it was clear to me that I would ultimately sell all of the assets that had come under my responsibility, including the bank. I felt then that my soul was in giving to the community, in philanthropy, in charity, in transformation, in world peace.

Since I knew that in order to bring peace to the world we must, first and foremost, achieve inner peace, I commissioned an international study to check ways and means of facilitating this change. We examined programs for rehabilitating prisoners, educational programs in schools, drug and alcohol rehabilitation programs, and more. After about a year and a half of searching and review, I realized that all of the methods—both conventional and alternative—are used in Israel. Since I believe that each of us can attain inner peace, and is personally responsible for this, I understood that my contribution is to spread the message and to make the path to change more accessible. But which path to choose? Each person is entitled to choose the path that is most suitable and correct for him. Therefore, I decided to create a pluralistic organization that includes representation of and references to these numerous methods and various paths. Through this organization, each person can choose what best suits him, can find his path to inner peace, and thus plant the seeds for world peace. This is how the Essence of Life organization was created. It is a nonprofit organization that is entirely financed from the family's funds via the Ted Arison Family Foundation and works to raise awareness and provide tools for inner peace, in accordance with the vision we formulated.

Essence of Life

OUR CALLING: **World peace.**

OUR PURPOSE: **Returning humankind to its essence.**

OUR MISSION: **Bringing about a major shift in collective consciousness.**

OUR CORE VALUES: **Oneness, Love, Respect, Integrity, Honesty, Responsibility.**

Strategy

TARGET AUDIENCE: **Humanity, individuals, and organizations (governmental, public, private, business, and philanthropic, in Israel and worldwide).**

VALUE: Leadership out of a mission of love, accuracy, and clarity; spiritual pluralism out of free choice.

STRATEGIC FOCUS: To synchronize the message and conduct of everyone in the organization at any given time.

STRATEGIC PROMISE: Being it.

STRATEGIC INTENT: Teaching ourselves as individuals and as a society a new language, a language of the soul, the heart and the body, which will generate a fundamental change in our society.

During that period, I went on a business tour with the Israeli minister of communications to the city of Ariel, which was related to the communications company the group owned at the time. We saw a presentation by the mayor, and when I told him about Essence of Life, he was very enthusiastic and proposed that I launch the program there. The organization was just beginning, and the details of its operation were not yet clear, but the mayor was persistent and for the next three months continued to make this offer until I agreed. This was the breakthrough and first stage of Essence of Life. We started out without knowing exactly what we were getting ourselves into, but everyone involved had a lot of desire, a lot of faith, and a great sense of mission. We knew that we were bringing something new to the State of Israel and, subsequently, to the entire world. We started working on the content for children and teenagers, which included a book, a play, a training kit for teachers, and storytellers for kindergartens. We also worked on a television series and built an Internet site for adults, children, and teenagers in Hebrew and English, which will be expanded in the future to include other languages. We later began operating the Essence of Life radio station, and we are working on an exhibit that will express the values of Essence of Life and the vision of the entire Arison Group.

Those were unbelievable days. There was a lot of work to be done, and also quite a few difficulties. At the height of that period, I was introduced to a channeler who told me, among other things, that I would soon have a difficult experience with the media.

"You'll feel like you're standing in front of a firing squad, but you won't die," she told me. Despite the fact that I had not asked her for the channeling and even felt that she had invaded my privacy without my consent, everything that she told me came to pass. Two weeks after this meeting, there was a press conference in which I defended the bank after it fired 900 employees.

No one knew at the time that I had nothing to do with the layoffs. The controlling shareholder is not involved in the daily affairs of the bank, and the layoffs were the decision of the CEO, the management, the chairman, and board of directors, who informed me just prior to the announcement. Even today, in retrospect, I do not necessarily think that their decision was wrong, but I know that I would have done it differently. The layoffs generated a wave of slander against the bank, and against me in particular. Since this was the moment when the Essence of Life campaign—"Peace Starts Within Me"—was launched, many people unfortunately saw a contradiction between the fact that I, on the one hand, talk about peace and, on the other hand, fire employees. I convened a press conference to sound my voice, to explain my intention, but without success. Standing before the media was very hard for me, and I felt attacked, hated, and misunderstood. And still, I felt that there was a reason for this test, and that the exposure I received, as negative as it was, served a purpose: it made me a public figure, gave me a platform, and when the right moment came, I would be able to use this platform to convey the messages that I believe in. For this purpose, I was ready to stand up to anything they threw at me. What I did not understand then is that we have the power to create our reality. We can create the world in which we live and choose what is right for us—not only to use the opportunities that cross our paths, but to create for ourselves the opportunities that suit us.

On the other hand, this was a period of joy in my personal life. I met my third husband and felt great happiness. I was on top of the world. But the tests did not stop. Soon after our marriage in 2003, as I was recuperating at home from minor surgery, my husband suddenly disappeared. Until that moment, he had cared for me with a devotion I had never seen, and was constantly at my side. Therefore, I did not understand what happened. But when he returned home after several long hours, broken, it turned out that the nurse who took care of me had accused him of sexual harassment and that he had been taken to the police for interrogation. Since I was a witness to what had occurred, I knew that this accusation was false.

It was clear to me that we needed to get away a bit from the tempest raging around us, and we went sailing on the yacht. Then, we received more bad news—the money of the entire family and the inheritance of my children were in danger. One of my attorneys called to tell me that the State of Israel was about to amend tax legislation to enable it to take part of my assets in the United States, assets that were never in Israel. It was absurd. On the one hand, the government tries to encourage Jews to immigrate to Israel. But when Zionist Jews, who do not need to be encouraged and do not require assistance, come to Israel—and invest, contribute, facilitate change, and create work places—the government makes it hard for them. The attorney explained to me that if I choose to live in Israel, the decision would have a detrimental effect on the rest of my family, whether they live in Israel or not. I did not know what to do.

There was a police investigation being conducted against my husband, accusations and more accusations. It was impossible to walk down the street because of the hateful looks from people. A harsh feeling of evil and rampant gossip prevailed. And what about the children—my son David, who was then in the army, my daughter Cassie, my son Jason, who was traveling at the time, Daniel, my youngest son, and my husband's daughters? I was in the midst of some important moves in the field of business and in philanthropy. How could we pack up an entire life at a moment's notice? We decided to fly to New York for consultation. We sat together, the entire family, including Daniel's father, in the attorneys' offices, surrounded by thirty advisors from Israel and the United States, and they all implored us to leave Israel.

I took the opportunity to attend a large gathering with the Dalai Lama. During his lecture, I received a message from above: "Everyone can connect directly to God. There is no longer a need for gurus, rabbis, or priests." I was told that my role is to show people that everyone can directly connect to God, without intermediaries. I did not want to live in the

United States, and I knew that if I remained, I would not be able to fulfill the mission I had started to carry out in Israel. I was torn, but there was no alternative, and after ten days of discussion we decided to move to Miami, temporarily.

We were advised to shut down the Arison foundation in Israel, to remain in Miami, and most importantly, not to tell anyone what was happening or why. And that is what we did. I closed the foundation for the time being, but helped to find jobs for everyone in one of my other organizations, such as Essence of Life and Matan. I did this without revealing my plans to anyone because I knew that I would want to reopen the foundation when I returned to Israel. Meanwhile, in the Israeli press, I was quoted as saying things I had never said. They claimed that I said that Israel is an ungrateful country and that we had fled from the police investigation. These claims were totally false. I did not speak with the media and did not respond to anything.

We moved the entire family to Miami and stayed there for nine months, during which I sat, gazed at the wonderful view, and cried.

I knew that I would do anything to return to Israel.

And then I was hit with another blow. I was falsely accused of kidnapping my youngest son and was being blackmailed. Since I did not give in to this extortion, I found myself in court, dealing with heaps of lies. The experience was sobering and shocking for me. Everything I heard there was lies, but I only told the truth. My attorney told me, "No one tells the truth in court. Everyone lies, and the judge must decide who lies better." I was completely stunned by this statement. It was a difficult time in every way. My relationship with my husband deteriorated as he began to engage more and more in material matters, and I delved more and more into spiritual matters. When he had to return to Israel due to unfortunate family circumstances, I had to remain in the United States because of the trial. I could not be with him at that difficult moment and support him, and he was also not there to support me at the court hearing. The media trumpeted his absence, completely blew it out of proportion and gave it far-reaching interpretations. A warrant was issued prohibiting my son from leaving the narrow confines of Miami, and when we watched television, we saw that in Israel they were continuing to sling false and distorted accusations against us. But we were helpless. There was nothing we could do.

It was a difficult pregnancy. We were in the United States for nine months—nine months of weeping, of sadness, of frustration. Nine months followed by a birth that was no less difficult. We finally reached an agreement that enabled us to return to Israel, but not to peace and quiet. Instead, we faced a long trial conducted against my husband. I was sure that justice would prevail, but I was wrong. He went to prison despite his innocence. Our love and spirituality were what helped us during this period. My faith and his rare strength enabled us to deal with the media, and with the gazes of those around us.

I realized that there is no justice, that there cannot be justice in the current system, wherever it may be. Justice must start with each and every one of us, because no one can really know another person when we barely know ourselves. Only after a person does inner consciousness work does he understand and see himself. So how could any judge know the truth that resides in the heart of another person? Indeed, the judge is sometimes surrounded by media that besieges him and feeds him with lies. Perhaps social and environmental pressures are exerted upon him. And this is without even mentioning his human desire for personal advancement. This was a hard lesson for me, and I think that one of the greatest pains in my life was the pain of injustice I was exposed to in the court system, the State Prosecutor's Office, and the police.

At the time, and perhaps as a result of the difficulties in my personal life, a significant change occurred in my business philosophy. Before we temporarily moved to Miami, I wanted very much to sell all of my businesses. I felt that I was being faithful to my father's memory, and held and maintained all of what he had bequeathed to me, but these were his dreams, his people, his way, his desires and visions. And where was I? I felt deeply the burden of responsibility as the controlling shareholder in a bank that serves one-third of Israel's population. The condition and activity of the bank touches upon every family and, to a considerable extent, the economy of the country depends on it. There are people who have a hard time understanding this responsibility, this burden. They tend to see only the profits, not the loans that must be repaid. They see the control and do not understand that this is a hollow definition because the legislation and strict regulation turn it into control without control. I tried to search myself, honestly and directly, to see whether this is what I wanted. Do I want this headache? Do I want to be attacked by the media? Do I want the distress I feel when I receive letters from people who blame me for their difficulties? Is this what I want? I am a good person, why do I need to be in a situation in which people think bad things about me?

But despite all the positive things I did at the bank, and despite the fact that I brought to the bank values of respect for the customer and giving to the community, and that I had managed to make the best of the situation, I felt: That's it. Enough.

But when I returned to Israel, I understood that the fact that I had thought about selling the bank countless times and yet had not done so was not coincidental. I began to understand that the business world is no less important than philanthropy, and perhaps even more so. It means investment in the State of Israel, creating employment for thousands of people, livelihoods for countless families. I realized that the bank is part of my mission, that there is a reason I am here, that I have a platform from which I can create change that can influence, in ever-expanding circles, the country and the world. It is perhaps a difficult burden, but I have a purpose, and I must fulfill it.

So I returned to Israel feeling empowered, focused, and more connected to myself. It was clear to me that I could not allow people to threaten me and to try to divert me from my path.

I decided not to sell the bank, but I thought that I would sell the rest of the companies that remained, such as Shikun & Binui, a global real estate and infrastructures company. I started the process, but then, a moment before finalizing the sale, I received a very clear message, which I did not understand at the time, not to sell. I decided to follow this message and did not sell the company because my experience has taught me to rely not only upon my business intuition and not only on economic logic, but to also take into account the spiritual aspect. Time has proven that this was a correct decision on every level.

One of the first steps I took in pursuing my new path was to part ways with the manager who had worked at my father's side and helped me during the period I define as the inheritance period, a time of honoring my father and his memory. I sat and met with my coach, after years of not seeking his assistance, and embarked again on a journey of a new vision. I wanted to formulate for myself a general outlook, a worldview that includes both business and philanthropy, and not to see them as separate entities, but to know that, in my eyes, they share a single overall goal.

Earlier, I had engaged in vision work by myself with the coach, but this time I included three senior managers, and together we developed the vision. Indeed, it was clear to me that the moment my managers, who are also company directors, participated in the process of discovering the vision and connecting to it, they would be able to lead the process of implementing the vision in each individual company, because it would be part of them. I knew that in the past it was difficult for me to formulate a vision and that the process took a long time. Therefore, I was surprised that despite the hard work, we managed to reach a vision within a short period of time.

The Arison Group's Vision

CALLING: **To secure the human existence.**

PURPOSE: **To bring about a higher consciousness worldwide.**

MISSION: **Setting the ground for a new reality on Earth for the entire universe, and creating a reality based on perfect balance and harmony.**

CORE VALUES: **Responsibility, Alignment, Leadership, Creation, Being it.**

We worked on strategy, tactics, and goals, and then continued on to develop the vision for Arison Investments.

Arison Investments

CALLING: To invest in securing the human existence.

PURPOSE: To bring about a higher business consciousness.

MISSION: Setting the ground for a new business reality on earth.

CORE VALUES: Responsibility, Leadership, Integrity, Being, Support, and Directing.

Strategy

STRATEGIC INTENT: Business investments intended to bring added value to Israel and the world.

TARGET AUDIENCE: Stakeholders—decision-makers, policy makers, partners, market players, clients, suppliers, future generations.

ADDED VALUE: Reputation of integrity and business impeccability.

VALUES TO STAKEHOLDERS: Integrity, transparency, human caring, combined with global influence and resonating inner strength.

STRATEGIC FOCUS: **First of all, to bring benefit to humanity, and only then to grow and profit, and not the opposite.**

STRATEGIC PROMISE: **Accurate and clear intention and planning.**

KEY STRATEGIC RESULT: **Implementation of new investments and conversion of existing investments to bring about added value to the environment and humanity within a few years. Changing the values, conduct, and language of the organization within a few years.**

I started to review each of the companies and entities I owned, including both businesses and philanthropic enterprises. I decided that I would part with whatever was inconsistent with the vision and would adapt whatever could suit it, and that I would acquire, develop, or add whatever was lacking.

The philanthropic organizations matched the vision perfectly. The Arison Foundation contributes to enhance the quality of life and insists on giving people fishing poles rather than fish; Essence of Life promotes world peace via inner peace. Over time, I also established a new philanthropic organization, All One, which grew out of Essence of Life and was born from the understanding that we are all connected, that there is a connection between all of humanity, that what occurs on one side of the planet affects the other side, and that for the sake of securing human existence we all must understand and act from the perspective that we are all part of One.

All One

CALLING: **We are all one.**

PURPOSE: **To generate a global conversation of a new reality; Oneness consciousness.**

MISSION: **To think and act with the understanding that we are all part of One, everywhere on the planet.**

CORE VALUES: **Responsibility, Love, Respect, Mutual Responsibility.**

Strategy

STRATEGIC PROMISE: **Unity exists when people act from Oneness consciousness.**

STRATEGIC FOCUS: **To be in Oneness consciousness, when each person is connected to his uniqueness.**

ADDED VALUE: **Achieving clarity and accuracy within a pure heart.**

STRATEGIC INTENT: **To raise collective consciousness.**

STRATEGIC RESULT: **Mainstream; a critical mass of people who understand the All One consciousness.**

The Arison Group also adopted the Ruach Tova (Good Spirit) organization, which works to bring people closer together by encouraging and coordinating voluntarism and mutual assistance. The organization specializes in matching those seeking to volunteer with people who could benefit from their time and assistance. Ruach Tova also coordinates the activities of Good Deeds Day, which I initiated. It is a day on which each person is asked to do a good deed for someone else, no matter how small, because even one person's smile is a good deed that echoes onwards. Good Deeds Day has become a day that facilitates giving in every form, and a special Internet site was set up to coordinate all of the day's activities. Through this site, people can join one of the many various projects listed and participate in the way that best suits them.

Matan—Your Way to Give is also continuing along the path I charted for it. And despite the fact that it operates independently and is not a part of the Arison Group, it also makes its contribution to the great vision.

In business, we reached the conclusion that beyond the investment in securing human existence, we would invest only in areas that bring added value to Israel and to the world. We started on a campaign to develop visions for the business entities, to part with entities that did not match the vision, such as several high-tech companies that were still under the group's ownership, and to locate businesses in which I wanted to invest. Of course, it is a complex task to develop a vision in public business. Each of the companies, whether private or public, stands on its own. Each of them has a board of directors, management, employees. I do not interfere in everyday management. The most significant way in which I can influence the companies that are under my responsibility is by means of my vision.

It is important to make clear that, first and foremost, a business must be profitable. I have a responsibility to the shareholders, customers, employees, and, of course, to myself. As I have already stated, the companies have loans to repay, and I also want to make a profit, a good one. But no less important to me, and perhaps even more, are the vision and the added value.

About ten years ago, I tried to develop a vision for Shikun & Binui that I called Apartments of Light. I wanted to make it possible for people to live in apartments that would have an abundance of light and large windows; apartments that would convey a good feeling, surrounded by greenery; apartments built with consideration for the environment, in harmony with nature; apartments that constitute a bridge to peace. Ten years ago, my vision was not realized. I was not strong enough. But this time, I approached the task equipped with will, strength, and an understanding of my mission. People in the company still did not understand how

I came to wish for sustainable construction, green and ecological building, but my determination and that of my managers helped me very much. Al Gore's film *An Inconvenient Truth* opened the eyes of many who had not understood me. Suddenly, people woke up and saw that these are precisely the things I had been talking about for ten years already. And once they understood, we could start to lead in this field with a new vision, written by the management and the board of directors.

Shikun & Binui

CALLING: **A leading business group that creates a sustainable and advanced environment in Israel and around the world.**

PURPOSE: **To lead a sustainable business environment with global power that combines excellence, innovation, humanity, and social responsibility/accountability.**

CORE VALUES: **Responsibility, leadership, integrity, transparency, humanity, and mutual respect.**

FORMATIVE PRINCIPLES: **Leadership, creation of a sustainable environment, social responsibility, comprehensiveness, fostering human assets, teamwork.**

This experience taught me an important lesson: not to give up on my vision, on my truth, on what I believe in, even if people do not understand me, even if there is resistance. After I saw so many of the messages and channelings I received come true, I understood that in many cases I am ahead of my time. I understood that I had received a message not to sell Shikun & Binui. Now its vision was adapted to securing human existence and leading sustainable construction in the world. Of course, this is not a vision that can be completely realized overnight, and there will always be those who criticize and only see what is not perfect. Such processes take time, a lot of time, and the important thing is the fact that we have embarked on our journey. I have complete confidence that Shikun & Binui will ultimately be a 100% sustainable company, which does not harm the environment and, in fact, does just the opposite.

At the same time, Arison Investments began to review companies working in the field of sustainability. This was a particularly complex review because, in response to newspaper advertisements, we received a large number of proposals, all of which we needed to examine. But ultimately, a number of options for investment were proposed to me in all sorts of areas, from solar energy to wind energy (Shikun & Binui eventually decided to enter these fields), geothermic energy, and more. In the meantime, one word started to resonate within me: water, water, water. I decided that this is what I want to invest in. I felt that while we are living with a sense of scarcity, there is an abundance of water in the world, an abundance we must protect and realize. I appointed an expert in the field and, together with the senior managers, we began to create the new company's vision. This was the first vision I developed for a business organization in which I was aware, from the beginning to end, that everything came from above and was channeled through me.

Miya—The Water Initiative of Arison Investments

CALLING: Securing the existing water abundance in the world.

PURPOSE: Global leadership in creation and development of solutions for actualization of water abundance worldwide.

MISSION: To invest in securing the actualization of the existing water abundance worldwide and the power of pure water.

CORE VALUES: Leadership, integrity and trustworthiness, responsibility and accountability, excellence, innovation.

Strategy

STRATEGIC INTENT: Pure intent–Pure water
Creation, integration, and management of existing practical and doable solutions.

Target Audience : Water suppliers in Israel and worldwide, influential and active participants in the world of water in Israel and worldwide.

Values to Stakeholders/Added Value:
- Leadership and innovative perspective in the world of water.
- Local and global strength.
- The ability to create, integrate, and manage practical and doable existing solutions.
- First-rate management team.
- Pure intent.
- Reputation of integrity and business impeccability.
- Innovative technology for the world of water.
- Long-term commitment.
- Committed to Earth's sustainability.

Strategic Focus: Everything is solvable.

Market Promise: Everything exists.

The name of the company, Miya, is one of the seventy-two names of God in the Kabbalah and means "from God." And while there were some people in the company who preferred that I not emphasize the profound meaning I find in the company's name, I feel with all my soul that it is a company of God, a company of the new world, of the world of tomorrow. Realization of the company's potential will connect humanity to the abundance and help to ensure the human existence. In a speech I gave at the launch of Miya in Vienna, in 2007, I wanted to emphasize the importance of fulfilling the earth's abundance of water:

I believe that through the combination of business and philanthropy, it is possible to influence and bring about change on a global level, regardless of national and political borders, and to lead towards a better environment and reality on earth. In today's world, we all have a responsibility to generate change. And via our leadership, we will be able to create a better world because, unlike countries, business and philanthropic initiatives have no borders.

I feel a personal responsibility and obligation to do everything in my power to lead toward a better future for us and for the generations to come.

As a business entity that invests in and impacts all vital facets of life—finance, real estate and infrastructures, water and energy—we are developing management strategies that take a comprehensive, long-term view of all the aspects: economic, social, and environmental.

By pursuing a long-term vision, we will be able to also imbue others with the passion to generate change in all of the areas in which we invest.

We provide a response to universal human needs, from which we derive business potential as well as added value for the human race.

Water is a universal human need, an essential resource for all life systems; water is a universal challenge that offers, as I see it, an opportunity for business innovation and a beneficial effect upon the entire world. We at the Arison Group believe the world is entitled to enjoy an abundance of water, and certainly not be suffering from scarcity.

Throughout history, nations, peoples, and tribes have fought over water. Research shows that one-fifth of the world's population has no access to clean, pure water.

We look at the earth's resources, and we see abundance, an abundance of water. And on the other hand, we see highly ineffective utilization of this precious and essential resource. We see the loss of huge amounts of water. Here, precisely, lies the supreme importance of Miya, a global company whose extensive activity is intended to maximize the utilization of the world's existing abundance of water and to become a global leader in the creation and development of solutions for attaining this goal.

This is exactly what impelled me to establish Miya and to create for it a vision with a business outlook that brings added value to the State of Israel and the entire world. Miya, with its cutting-edge expertise and technology that rank among the world's leaders, will provide solutions for fully utilizing the earth's abundance of water, thus doing its part to secure the human existence.

Another word that resonates frequently within me is "purity." And so, I examined possibilities in the field of air purification. I believe that everyone, everywhere in the world, deserves to breathe clean air, and this conviction grew stronger after I visited Vietnam and Cambodia. Even before I landed there, I received a message that instructed me to care for clean air in the world. But when I arrived, I understood in full what it means to live in a place where it is impossible to breathe, where people have to walk around with masks because of air pollution.

Another field that I am examining and which is close to my heart is related to the subject of energy: clean energy. I am not looking merely for alternative energy that is less polluting. I believe that completely clean energy is possible because I believe wholeheartedly that everything we can think or dream of exists. Perhaps we have not found or invented it yet, but it exists.

My strong desire to find a company to create a solution for clean energy for transportation, for the air pollution produced by the use of cars, planes, and ships (a field I know through the family business), derives from my personal sense of responsibility, as a private individual, as a businesswoman, and as part of humanity.

The Arison Group includes businesses and public companies, and we must first and foremost look at the economic aspect of everything we do. But if we examine the aspects of a business deal and discover that it will have negative consequences, we will not go forward with it because, in the long term, we will not derive any profit from it. On the contrary, if we sustain the world, we will also sustain ourselves. If the world profits, then we will profit too. Money in itself is not sufficient, and we see this clearly today. The banks throughout the world that allowed money to be their sole guide and did not have a moral position, collapsed. The money did not save them. It ruined them.

As I have already pointed out, I am prohibited from interfering in the daily operations of a public company like the bank. I completely accept this prohibition since the things that truly interest me are not at all related to the managerial decisions but rather to the essential aspects: the vision, the values, the integrity, and also, of course, the profitability. The way I can make sure that these aspects are addressed is by choosing a chairperson and mobilizing the board of directors for my vision—by choice and out of a recognition that this is for the good of the bank. The vision for the bank was the most challenging vision to formulate and one of the most crucial ones due to the enormous importance of the bank for the Israeli economy, the number of employees, and the families that depend on it. When I started to see the bank's vision in my mind's eye, I received a message about "creating financial freedom." I decided that I wanted to mobilize the bank to serve as an example for financial institutions in the world, to promote its clients towards a situation in which they are not dependent on the bank but are instead partners of it. This is because I believe that any relationship based on dependency is a distorted relationship. Dependency is a phenomenon that harms both the person who is dependent and the person he is dependent upon. It is a phenomenon that causes hatred and anger, as I already noted in regard to national security. And this is a fact that I have found to be true at all levels: personal, interpersonal, financial, national, and more.

When I brought the message I received to the chairman of the bank, I learned that the management had started to offer the public financial know-how. The bank can use the information at its disposal to help its clients better understand the possibilities and paths available to them. The know-how and the freedom came together, and the management and board of directors formulated the bank's vision.

Bank Hapoalim

VISION: **To strive to be a global and leading financial institution, based in Israel, focused on its customers and working to achieve their financial freedom.**

We operate to maximize the value for the stakeholders in congruence with our sustainability principles—economic, social, and environmental. We are committed to fostering human resources and encouraging excellence and innovation.

We act based on core values of humanity, integrity, openness, and responsibility.

Today, in light of the global economic crisis, the principles of financial know-how and financial freedom are more important than ever. When I tried to say things along those lines several years ago, people ridiculed me. They said that I wanted to give money to people who would not repay it. No one understood that I was speaking about knowledge, tools, and responsibility—the responsibility of the bank towards its customer, as well as the customer's responsibility for the commitments he takes upon himself. When the bank demonstrates responsibility towards the customer and provides him with financial know-how, the customer has tools for making the right choice. Only then is a partnership created, because when we give people tools for making the right choice, we gain a partner, which inspires both sides rather than having them face off as strong versus weak, knowledgeable versus powerless.

Many people hate banks and do not understand why they need to pay them. They have misconceptions about the purpose and function of the bank. A bank provides a product, just like any other business. The product the bank provides is money. A person who buys clothes in a store is ready to pay much more than the cost of manufacturing. But when it comes to banking, people are angry when they are required to pay for the product they purchase and the service they receive. The role of the bank is to teach, assist, and serve, to provide the know-how and the tools, to lead its clients to financial freedom. I want our customers to have knowledge, power, and the ability to properly choose and decide, to create a partnership with the bank, and not to be dependent upon it.

The global economic crisis resulted from a banking system that did not recognize responsibility, which was guided not by the good of the customer, but by greed. It took more and more for itself at the customer's expense. This was the approach in the United States: the banks pushed people, some of whom did not understand what they were taking upon themselves, into taking loans. And now the entire world is paying the price for the customer's misunderstanding and the lack of responsibility on the part of these banks. Greed cannot prosper over time. Only responsibility can lead to prosperity. Only morality can bring success. If we allow ourselves to be led by greed, the desire to sell more and more, without taking an interest in what this is doing to people, without caring whether they will collapse or die, then we too shall collapse and die.

This truth applies to all areas. For years, the world has operated out of greed. We took from one another, we took from nature, we took from the environment—and now, we are forced to deal with the consequences, with the wars over territory, with the economic collapse, with the air pollution, with the destruction of the environment, with the global warming.

We have worked hard to strengthen the position of the businesses in the group. We have issued bonds, organized loans and bank financing, acquired a controlling share of Shikun & Binui from the employees, and stabilized the controlling share in the bank by acquiring the holdings of the American partners and Israel Salt Industries, a public company that we turned private. When we acquired the company, only one thing interested me beyond the wisdom of the business move: whether the company's manufacturing processes are harmful to nature. The study we conducted indicated that the company does not damage the environment, and that the opposite is true. Eventually, I began to understand that this acquisition had much wider significance. Salt is a mineral of vital importance. Without salt, there is no life. And indeed, the word "vitality" later began to resonate within me. The company is now in the process of developing a vision, and I have no doubt that this vision will include attention to vitality or life.

The acquisition of Israel Salt Industries was a good and correct business decision, but also an important step in realizing the group's vision.

After many years in which I wrote and pursued various visions, I had a revelation: I saw how all of these different and separate visions together create a model, a model of a new world, a pure, clean, and true world. It is a model that provides a template for every company or organization that seeks to lead in a different way, or realize its human potential, for the entire world. It is a model that deals not only with the economic aspects, but presents the moral, ethical, and spiritual aspects within each company or community, down to its last individual—because it is only these individuals who can forge a new, true, and authentic leadership.

This model must address all levels because in the new world it will no longer be possible to look at things separately. It is not enough, for example, only to be concerned with our surroundings. We must address all layers at all levels— personal, interpersonal, communal, and environmental— and the language we use is the backbone of this outlook. I wanted us to learn, personally and as a group, a new language—a language of the soul, of the heart, and of the body, which will lead to significant change in society, a unifying language of awareness and experience, a truly global discussion. This is because a language is not merely words and body language. It is energy, and everything a person conveys echoes in expanding circles. Each vision is a brick. The language is the mortar that connects the bricks into a single structure, into one model.

Based on this approach, we developed a department that serves all of the group's members, business and philanthropic alike, in all things related to language and communications. We also contributed to the Center for Awareness Communication at the Interdisciplinary Center Herzliya, an Israeli university.

Shari Arison

Vision of the Shari Arison Center for Awareness Communication

CALLING: Creating a better world, moral commitment, and opportunity for personal, interpersonal, and collective transformation.

PURPOSE: True and authentic self-expression.

MISSION: Collective responsibility of the media in Israel and worldwide.

CORE VALUES: Love, Responsibility, Integrity, Respect, Mutual Accountability.

STRATEGY: A mission to create a better world. Communication leadership.

STRATEGIC INTENT: Media people acting with responsibility and personal awareness, interpersonal and collective.

TARGET AUDIENCE: The world of media.

ADDED VALUE: Multidisciplinary research, international experts, international connections,

ethical content conveyed via knowledge and experience, groundbreaking technologies.

STRATEGIC FOCUS: **Awareness.**

When I began putting the model together, it was clear to me that I should not develop it alone or with a small group of senior executives, as I had done so far. Such a unifying model requires cooperation and input from each of the group's companies and organizations, and it was very important for me that my adult children participate as well, since they will follow in my footsteps in the future. The chairpersons and CEOs, the financial managers, my children, and the personal aides, everyone came together to embark on a new road, to build the vision of visions. The first meeting was a disaster. No one understood me. No one understood my vision, what I was trying to achieve, the new world that I was trying to create. Everyone resisted, and I got angry at everyone.

They wanted me to compromise. But how can you compromise on something that you believe in with all your heart and soul? Indeed, if Martin Luther King Jr. had compromised, we would not have a black president in the

White House today. If John F. Kennedy had compromised, mankind would not have made it to the moon. I felt tormented. They suggested that I try to develop the model by myself, but I knew that this was not the way, that the new world depends on togetherness, and not on aloneness. It was clear to me that I should not give up my principles, and that I did not want anyone else to give up his or hers. I wanted us to put the clay in the middle of the table and to knead it together. And so we did—with hard work, with everyone's truth, and with help from the founder of the language of Ahava Raba, which provided us the tools for connecting the conscious and subconscious of each of us to reach the truth. The process was not easy, but the journey was fascinating. And in the end, the definitions for the model were formulated.

The Shari Arison Model

ADDED VALUE FOR HUMANITY: **The courage and ability to lead to a better world by connecting between thought, emotion, and actions, and the fulfillment of the universal potential.**

WE ARE ALL ONE: Each person has his or her uniqueness. All of us comprise the whole and constitute part of it.

SUSTAINABILITY: Protecting and enhancing existence through economic, social, and environmental balance—for us and for the generations to come.

ABUNDANCE: Recognizing that everything exists and responsible action for ensuring "what is."

VOLUNTEERING: Action in the community, based on inner strength and love for others.

INNER PEACE: An internal, personal, continuous, and constant process that leads us to a quiet place, balanced and tranquil within us.

GIVING: To give from a sincere, empowering, and true place.

FINANCIAL FREEDOM: The freedom (and the desire) to choose, based on responsibility and understanding of the framework of abilities and economic possibilities at any given moment.

LANGUAGE AND COMMUNICATION: A range of channels that facilitate the sending and receiving of information, with synchronization, authenticity, respect, and precision, which lead to an understanding of the messages as they are.

VITALITY: An internal, driving energy that enables a dynamic pace of life, vibrancy, and constant renewal.

PURITY: The clarity of thoughts, intentions, and actions.

FULFILLMENT: Realizing the self's full potential (while being at peace with our choices).

BEING: Harmonious existence with all of the components that create the whole.

But before we had a chance to get to the strategy and tactics of the model, the world around me went crazy. I suddenly found myself dealing with attacks on all fronts—personal, interpersonal, financial, and political. The Bank of Israel, the regulator, which wields enormous power, demanded that I fire the chairman of Bank Hapoalim, but despite my repeated requests, I did not receive a reason that justified this step. I was surrounded by lies, manipulations, and leaks to the press, and an all-out war was waged against me. Even the media served as a pawn in the hands of those who rose up to destroy me. Many people did not understand why I was not willing to sacrifice the chairman in order to gain some peace and quiet, but I refused to be untrue to myself and was not willing to lie—not to myself, and not to those around me.

I promised that I would pursue the truth to the end and that I would support everyone who is with me—but only if they act with integrity, in unison, and with full cooperation, and that I would work to find a solution to this conflict without sacrificing the principles and the truth.

The forces that are rising against me, all of the destructive and belligerent energy they are radiating, derives from the old world, which is trying to defend itself from the change that is about to come.

The time has come to take leave of those whose actions are motivated by egoism and not by self-love and inner balance, from those who take pleasure in hedonism instead of connecting to the abundance. And I am now in the process of ending these relationships in all the circles around me, from the personal to the professional. This is the moment of truth. The time of the channeling I received many years ago has come. I must take the lead—not in the political arena of government but in a different kind of politics, of the people, of people who want things to change, and not in the way the familiar old leadership conducts itself, but in a new way, a way of action and personal example. I hope others will follow me and understand that we can bring about change only by connecting with ourselves, through truth and a growing togetherness, a togetherness of good.

The first signs of this change can already be seen, and people who opposed me and rose up against me in the past are today defending me and surrounding me with love. The circle is closing, and whatever is no longer appropriate for the new world is coming to its end.

A war of good and evil is raging around us. And while evil usually seemed to have the upper hand in the old world, I truly believe that the era of the new has arrived, and that it is the time when good will triumph.

Coming
Together

OUR SOUL IS INNATELY GOOD; ALL OF IT IS FREE AND TRANQUIL, PEACEFUL, LOVING, AND INFINITE. It always wishes to return to its divine source. The body wants to remain here. It wants to survive; it wants to live. These two forces, the physical and the spiritual, each pull in a different direction. For many years, I was connected to my soul. I wanted to continue onward. I was not happy here, in this body, on this earth, because I wanted to transform myself and move on. I ignored the fact that my soul had chosen a body in which to reside, that this body had a will of its own, and that there also has to be a place for this will. It must also find expression. These two elements must cooperate. We must achieve balance and harmony between the two forces that pull us, each in a different direction.

I have been asked many times why I do not enter politics, where ostensibly I could have a greater impact. But I feel that my calling and purpose in this world are to communicate my messages and help people achieve change. This is not simple. It takes time, and it requires that one person change himself, and then another person and another one.

We will never be able to bring everyone in the world to inner peace. Not all people want to reach their true essence. Inner consciousness work and soul-searching cannot be done through coercion, but only through will. Thus, the religions that preach coercion do not guide their believers towards their inner essence. The Ahmadinejads of the world, the Bin Ladens of the world, will not change their ways, regardless of how hard we try to explain to them that peace begins within them.

That's okay. We do not need them. We do not need every single person in the world. We only need enough. A critical mass of people who live in peace, in love, in acceptance, in respect, in light, would resonate throughout the world, and then the change would occur, as if overnight. Someone I met once illustrated the power of this critical mass via the image of a stadium. The stadium is completely dark. We cannot see anything, and no one can see the person standing next to him or even his own hands. And then, one person lights a candle. And another, and another. If enough people light a candle, it is sufficient to illuminate the stadium, to transform the darkness into light. There will always be people who surrender to the darker parts in themselves, who are full of evil and hatred. We cannot really change them, but we can change ourselves. But it is important to remember that we are not separate, each one to himself. All of us are part of the whole, the One, and every such change resonates. Each such change creates ripples, like a stone tossed into a pond. Each such change transforms the world.

This, in my view, is the profound meaning of the Talmudic verse, "…whoever saves one life is considered as if he had saved the entire world." There are those who think that this only refers to the soul of a Jew, because we are the chosen people, or that it entails saving the soul of someone else, external to us. But I believe that this soul we save must first of all be our own soul. Because if we save our own soul, the world will also be saved. And if we fall, the entire fabric of humanity will also be harmed.

My approach to the world came, first and foremost, from my intuition. My father, who was one of the greatest businessmen in the world and was asked by politicians to advise them on government activity in the field of economics, also relied on intuition. I am not saying that we do not need financial models and an academic perspective of the economy. Just as it is possible to make a consensual and formal peace between governments, as opposed to inner, true peace, it is also possible to conduct business via traditional economic notions. But as long as it remains only at this level, and we do not use intuition and emotion— essence—it will never be a new economy, an economy that adapts itself to the new world we face. It will remain only on the surface. This does not mean that someone who does business with the help of financial models and makes his decisions based on intellect, rather than emotion and intuition, will fail. But eventually, I believe that all businesses will have to change in order to succeed. Businesspeople will no longer be able to act in a rational, practical, and detached manner. There is power in the intellect, there is power in the heart, and there is power in the connection between the two. Nothing is separate. Everything is connected, and the moment the intellect and the heart work in tandem, the new economy will emerge.

The new economy is the connection between matter and spirit, the connection between the intellect, the emotion, and the soul. One of them can no longer come at the expense of the other. As long as these elements are separated from each other, we will also be separated from one another. Only a connection can bring harmony.

But this separation exists not only in the field of economics. It exists on all levels. People are separated from their hearts—not in the sense that we usually attribute to the heart, such as "love" or "generosity," but from the essence of themselves: from intuition, from values, from the inner connection. And the moment a person becomes connected to himself, he is actually connected to the entire world, because we are all one, we are all part of the whole, of God. The moment we ignore parts of the whole that is us or the whole that is the world, we harm both ourselves and the whole: If we ignore, for example, what our body is trying to tell us, we can become ill and collapse. And if we ignore air pollution, for example, we harm ourselves, the animals, the water, the land, the entire world. The focus on intellect, on the rational, was once very popular among businesspeople and in general. Where you studied and what you studied were very important. Today, people place a lot of emphasis on the body. How you look, what you eat, how much you exercise. There is not enough room for the spirit, for emotion, for the soul. To reach a balance, these elements must work together, in unison.

In order to better understand the new world, we must first understand the old world and the reasons for its collapse: as I have already pointed out, I believe that reality is a reflection of our inner essence. The war around us is a reflection of the inner war that exists in each of us, between good and evil. The global economic crisis is a reflection of something that is collapsing within us. Everything is found within us. Today, when there is a greater level of general awareness about matters involving the spiritual world, it is no longer possible to conceal the collapse and the inner war below the surface. Everything is rising. Everything is transparent and everything is a reflection. The external is the internal.

The natural disasters, the earthquakes, the tsunami, the forest fires, the floods—all of these are signs of a wound that is cleansing itself, of change that is occurring. As long as this involved nature, people could choose not to see the truth, the need for change. But the global financial crisis has led many people to internalize the fact that the old world no longer works. It is crumbling and making way for the new world. This is why many people are experiencing this crisis in a profound way, on an emotional level and even physically, even those who were not directly hurt by it. This is because we are all one, we are all connected to each other. Whether we know this or not, the connection exists. Therefore, we are all collapsing together. But from these difficult labor pains, a new world will be born.

The new world that I envision will be a clear, pure world. A world in which deception will not exist and truth will be possible. To reach the truth, we will need to remove the masks, refrain from fooling ourselves and making excuses: "I just don't want to hurt anybody," "I can't deal with it," "I don't have the energy," and so on.

The new economy will not be built on manipulation and will not only seek profits and the bottom line. It will be an empowering economy, built upon principles of cooperation and mutual responsibility. These principles will also guide the legal system, as well as the country's other systems. An economy based on these principles, on purity and truth, is also an economy that aims to succeed, to profit. But it must succeed and profit on additional levels, not only on the monetary one. And it must not act only to satisfy the egos of those taking part in it.

The new world and the new economy will be based on freedom for all. Freedom from the old. To achieve such freedom, we must find it first of all within ourselves. Only when one is aware, confident, and respects himself can he be truly liberated.

The old world lives in a consciousness of scarcity, of what is lacking. Therefore, the new world and the new economy will be based on abundance, internal abundance that will also lead to external abundance. The "have," the "what is" of the old world, which asks: "How much money do you have?" "How much property do you have?" actually stands for what is not, signifying a lack. A lack of confidence, a lack of faith in the true abundance, which asks: "How much light do you have?" The Kabbalah teaches us that we are a vessel, a vessel that can become full of light. As we remove more and more masks, more and more layers, from the intellectual, from the physical, the psychological and the spiritual, we will be able to shine more and more brightly. When a person wants, demands and takes only for himself, his "what is" creates a shortage and is created from shortage. But when a person makes room in his soul for receiving more and more light, he also radiates upon his surroundings and creates more of the "what is." Only then can he truly give. Not to give only to feel good about himself, to receive recognition, to please. This is not true giving. This is "to give in order to receive." To accept the fact of abundance and good in order to offer it to another is "to receive in order to give."

When I spoke at the annual General Assembly of the United Jewish Communities, Jewish Federations of North America, I tried to explain how I see the concept of *tikkun olam*, the transformation of the world, and our importance as a "vessel" according to the worldview of the Kabbalah:

Closing Speech - GA November, 2008

What is *tikkun olam*? For me, it encompasses infinite levels.

In my eyes, the most important step in transforming the world is the personal transformation of each and every one of us. It means stripping off all the masks and reaching the innermost truth—the essence. This may sound like a simple task, but it is what we spend our whole lives doing, whether consciously or subconsciously.

Layer upon layer weighs down on each one of us: insults, hurts, pressures, fears, and more. These layers, which stem from our childhood and even from various incarnations we've passed through, are the very layers we must peel away in order to be able to reach our essence and transform ourselves. In order to respect, we must respect ourselves. In order to love, we must love ourselves. And in order to reach peace, we must reach peace within ourselves.

As is taught in the Kabbalah, we are the vessel for receiving light, and the more light that enters our body, the more light we'll be able to give. Our body is our vessel. In order for the vessel to hold an abundance of light, it must be clean. This cleanliness means exactly the same as cleaning away the layers I spoke of before. In Judaism it is said that if you save one soul, it's as if you have saved the entire world. I think that the souls we must save are, first of all, each soul within oneself.

In my view, from the individual, we emerge into ever-widening circles: the interpersonal, family, community, environmental, national, and global.

When we speak of *tikkun olam* on the interpersonal level, we have much to learn before we can begin to teach. We need to learn to listen, to receive, to respect, and to love—truly. Mind, thoughts, words, talk, and actions must be synchronized. Sometimes we can smile at someone with our faces but kill him with the energy we emit. When words and actions contradict each other, we will not be able to perform *tikkun olam*, either in Israel or in the world.

On the issue of the environment, we see the effects and results of what we have done with our own hands. Nature is acting up, and not without reason. We must understand that we live on the earth and that it belongs to all of us. If we don't treat it responsibly, the results are foretold.

We live in a Jewish state, and we have a mission. Our mission is precisely this: transforming the world, *tikkun olam*. While this is our role, it is not about us; it is not for ourselves alone. Rather, it is for the entire world and all peoples, because this is our mission. When it is said that we are the Chosen People, this is what we were chosen for, to transform the world. And *tikkun olam* cannot be accomplished by issuing orders, by control, by arrogance. *Tikkun olam* can be done only by resonating authentic truth—each person with himself, with his family and his surroundings.

We, the Jewish People, have a mutual responsibility for each other and only together will we be able to accomplish our mission. If each one of us can understand his personal task and take responsibility for his own small portion of what God has given us, together we can carry out the mission of the Jewish world—*tikkun olam.*

I have given a lot during my lifetime. Whether it was during my childhood, when I gave my parents what they wanted of me, or the complete opposite of what they expected from me. Whether it was during my adult life, when I was always busy giving friends a place to stay, to be happy, to dance, to drink and eat, to give the house, the heart, the soul, to give money, to give time, and more. For a great many years, I gave without understanding that the source of my giving was wrong, without understanding that when we give it is not only important to know how much, to whom, and how. We must also know and understand why—what the desire or intention of the giver is. I did not realize that my giving, throughout my entire life, had come from a need to please, from a desire for people to love me, from the fact that I felt a victim, from a desire to be at the center of attention, from many incorrect and unclean reasons. True, I did not speak about or publicize the fact that I was giving because I did not want people to know. I always regarded this as modesty: I will give and not speak of it, and only I will know how much I give. But today I understand that deep down inside I wanted people to see, I wanted them to appreciate, I wanted to be at the center. And all the time, I felt exploited; I felt like a victim, I felt I was underappreciated. I felt that I was giving without receiving. I felt that people were biting off pieces of me, and I felt that I was selling my soul to please everyone. Today, after much inner consciousness work, I know that everything began with a little girl who wanted to be seen and to be loved. Today, I can understand the importance of the reason for true giving, and that true giving always begins with receiving. Receiving is much harder than giving.

The "what is not" is not necessarily expressed in a lack of money or resources. It can appear as a lack of love, of appreciation, of understanding, of confidence. Each person must identify what he lacks in essence and connect to the consciousness of the abundance within us, to see the "what is" and not the "what is not."

The scarcity, like the abundance, can grow. The more we focus on the "what is not," the more it grows and strengthens. The more we talk about poverty and scarcity, the more they grow. Our consciousness has power. Our attention has power. Our words have the power to create reality. And the more we focus this power on negative things, the more they rise and grow. It could be argued that the media, which in modern society has the greatest power, exerts the greatest influence on our attention, on our consciousness, that its words create our reality, and that it is to blame for amplifying the negative. The media is where we see and hear and read about all of the terrible things that happen in the world around us. For many years, when I was under attack by the media, I thought that it was to blame. But today, I know that the media is us. It reflects us, as people. If we are angry at yellow journalism for engaging only in gossip, we must first of all stop gossiping ourselves. It is not the media that sees bad things everywhere, but we who see what is bad. If each of us would engage in inner consciousness work, if each of us stopped being drawn towards hatred, pain and sadness, and started paying attention to what's good, clean and pure, this would be reflected outward, in the media and in the entire world.

I believe that the root of our problems, the problems of human beings, can be traced to a single seed— miscommunication. This miscommunication is ancient, accompanying us throughout our history, and is even perpetuated in myths like the Tower of Babel. Our communication with ourselves is flawed. We do not listen to our soul. We do not listen to our body. Or we listen to one at the expense of the other. And when the inner communication is flawed, it is clear that the communication with the outside also suffers. All the wars, conflicts, angers, insults—all spring from flawed communication. When we communicate through our shells, we cannot see because even if we speak to one another, deep down we are not connected to each other at all. This disconnection is blinding us. We do not see the Other, we do not understand that there is actually no such thing as hurting someone else: when we hurt another person, we are hurting ourselves.

I believe that we are all connected with each other, and that if we manage to see and recognize, to connect to the consciousness of One, we can truly create a new world. Globalization, and even negative events like the financial crisis, has proven to us how connected we are, how much each of us is part of the same body, which is the universe— a universe that is composed not only of humanity, but also of the environment in which we live. He who destroys the land, the air, the economy, the peace in a particular place, destroys them for everyone. And he who improves a particular place, improves it for everyone. Sadly, it is much easier for people to see and understand the negative impact of our connection. It is easier to see how the destruction of the rainforests affects people in the other hemisphere or how a real estate crisis in the United States affects Israel. But it is difficult for us to see the positive impact of our actions, of our personal responsibility. Why? Because this understanding, this vision, means that we are also obligated to do something. That it is in our own hands. Not only our future, but the future of the entire universe depends on it. The responsibility is personal, it lies upon the shoulders of each and every one of us. This is a very frightening thing to know.

Each one of us has potential, but the fulfillment of this potential is a matter of choice, of will. We must choose it, want it, work for it. It is sad and frustrating that many people choose not to fulfill themselves fully, whether or not they are aware of this.

The future is also filled with potential. I can see this potential taking shape, but the realization of the future is in our hands. It is our choice whether to make it happen.

Each of us can lead to a new world, to a positive world. Each is responsible for our future and, even now, each of us can make a commitment to change himself, his consciousness, his path, and his world.

Are you ready to pursue this path towards your self? Do you understand that when you connect to your essence, you will be connected to everything—to humanity, to nature, to God? If so, everything is in your hands. Get going. If you need assistance, ask for it sincerely and with faith. It will come. Yes, it will be difficult, but isn't it worth it?

Each and every one of you can make a change.

Acknowledgments

O<small>N MY PATH TO GIVING BIRTH TO THE NEW,</small> I <small>HAVE MET MANY PEOPLE, EACH OF WHOM MADE HIS CONTRIBUTION, GAVE FROM HIS UNIQUENESS AND ABILITIES, AND LEFT HIS MARK.</small> My thanks go to all of the people I list here. Perhaps they were not mentioned by name in this book, but their presence in it and in my life is very significant. I hope that I have not forgotten anyone, but if such an error has occurred, I apologize in advance and ask for your forgiveness.

Thank you from the bottom of my heart!

A: Uri Allony, Jason Arison, David Arison, Cassie Arison, Merav Atsits, Irit Atsmon, Tal Atsmon, Nahum Admoni, Orna Angel, Ron Asolin, Gideon Amichay.

B: Professor Gabi Barbash, Ravit Barniv, Eti Ben Ami, Einav Ben Haim, Avi Ben Shitrit, Nili Blum, Hanan Ben Yehuda.

C: Ed Case, Ram Caspi, Amir Cess, Rachel Cohen, Andrew L. Cohen.

D: Tovi Dahan, Alon Dankner, Dani Dankner, Shlomit De Vries, Iris Dror, Jim Dubin, Pnina Dvorin.

E: Rafi Elul, Shalom Elcott, Ofer Erdman, Shaul Elovitch.

F: Paul Fedorko, Jann Fisher, Aliza Fox, Tali Fridman.

G: Gabriella Gross, Baruch Gasol, Racheli Goldblatt, Tamar Goldberg, Dror Glazer, Benad Goldwasser.

H: Rami Hadar, Ya'el Ha'elyon (Blessed Memory), Liat Hayun-Bogin, Claudia Hanisch, Hanan Horowitz.

I: Irit Izakson, Aharon Menachem (Orni) Izakson.

J: Dadi Janki, Dianne Jaworski.

K: Tova Kalman, Zion Keynan, Moddi Keret, Ofer Kotler, Ruben Krupik, Silvia Kopitman, Hactor Kopitman, Richard Kohan, Moshe Koren.

L: Moshe Lahmani, Eran Laub, Ygal Lev, Sam and Michal Levi (Ahava Raba), Yudi Levy, Heddy Lewinsky, Ken Louie, Steve Lynch, Dr. Noam Lemelshtrich - Latar.

M: Noa Menhaim, Fred McNulty, Ziv Malkin, Rachel Meron, Barak Majar.

N: Mayor Ron Nachman, Shlomo Nehama.

O: John J. O'Neil, Hana Or, Booky Oren, Rabbi Eliyahu Ozrad.

P: Kobi Peer, Efrat Peled.

R: Kaynan Rabino, Ran Rahav, Professor Uriel Reichman, Shuki Reizel, Pini Rubin, Moshe Ribak, Tal Ronen, Maddy Rosenberg, Yoram Raved, Ariel Rosenberg.

S: Haim Samet, Daniel Sean, Shelly Schneider, Eran Shalev, Yuval Shamir, Jacob Schimmel, Dick Skor, Dan Smetanka, Gad Somekh, Jacob Steinmetz, Stan Steinreich, Ido Stern, Sharona Stillerman, Eliyahu Sviranovsky (Blessed Memory), Shalom Saar, Uri Shani, Jennifer Snyder, Gilead Sher.

T: Dovik Tal, Hanna Turjeman, Aviva Tamir, Yoram Turbowicz, Ofer Tzur.

V: Elia Velasquez, Uzi Vardizer.

W: Eileen Wackerstein, Richard S. Wagman, Dr. Brian Weiss, Meir Wietchner.

Y: Ahuva Yanai, Ilana Yashar, Uri Yehezkel, Udi Yerushalmi, Anat Yogev.

Z: Nir Zichlinskey, Shoshanna Zimmerman.

Thank you to the accountants, the advisors, the architects, the bankers, the broadcasters, the contractors, the customers, the directors, the engineers, the facilitators, the fitness trainers, the lawyers, the nutritionists, the partners, the producers, the storytellers, the suppliers, the teachers, the therapists, the trustees, the writers, and to my employees in Israel and all over the world, past, present, and future. All of you have a part in this birth.

Thank you to my father, Ted Arison, of blessed memory, my family, and my friends.

Thank you to everyone I have met along my path because each of them has taught me a lesson, each of them has reflected something within myself, especially my ex-husbands and Ofer, in particular, who taught me the joy of life and wholehearted laughter, the difference between hedonism and abundance, and between taking and receiving. In the time we shared together, I connected with my internal strength and discovered my true, authentic, and intimate wishes.

Thank you to the worlds above, to the guides and angels.

Thank you, God.